屋島之役

嗣信

主小代吴を

教經の

Dedicated to my late teacher,
Takashi Kawakami

BUSHIDO
EXPLAINED

The Japanese Samurai Code:
A New Interpretation for Beginners

ALEXANDER BENNETT

With Illustrations by **Baptiste Tavernier**

TUTTLE Publishing

Tokyo | Rutland, Vermont | Singapore

Contents

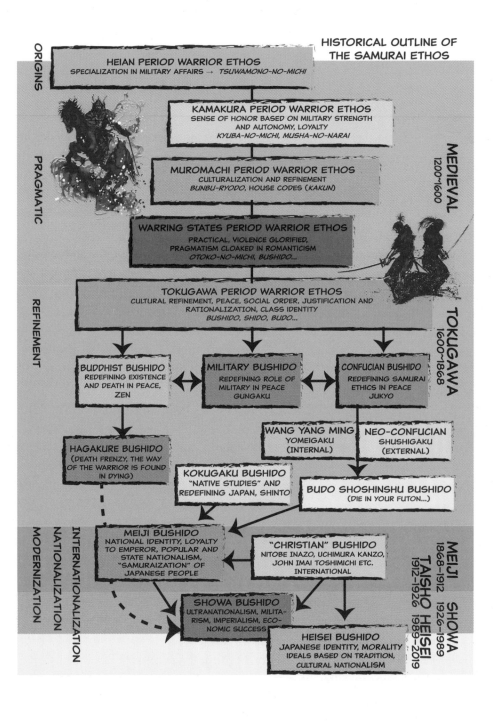

ORIGINS

PRAGMATIC

REFINEMENT

MODERNIZATION

INTERNATIONALIZATION
NATIONALIZATION

MEDIEVAL
1200~1600

TOKUGAWA
1600~1868

MEIJI
1868-1912

TAISHO
1912-1926

SHOWA
1926-1989

HEISEI
1989-2019

HEIAN PERIOD WARRIOR ETHOS
SPECIALIZATION IN MILITARY AFFAIRS → *TSUWAMONO-NO-MICHI*

KAMAKURA PERIOD WARRIOR ETHOS
SENSE OF HONOR BASED ON MILITARY STRENGTH
AND AUTONOMY, LOYALTY
KYUBA-NO-MICHI, MUSHA-NO-NARAI

MUROMACHI PERIOD WARRIOR ETHOS
CULTURALIZATION AND REFINEMENT
BUNBU-RYODO, HOUSE CODES (*KAKUN*)

WARRING STATES PERIOD WARRIOR ETHOS
PRACTICAL, VIOLENCE GLORIFIED,
PRAGMATISM CLOAKED IN ROMANTICISM
OTOKO-NO-MICHI, BUSHIDO...

TOKUGAWA PERIOD WARRIOR ETHOS
CULTURAL REFINEMENT, PEACE, SOCIAL ORDER, JUSTIFICATION AND
RATIONALIZATION, CLASS IDENTITY
BUSHIDO, SHIDO, BUDO...

BUDDHIST BUSHIDO
REDEFINING EXISTENCE
AND DEATH IN PEACE,
ZEN

MILITARY BUSHIDO
REDEFINING ROLE OF
MILITARY IN PEACE
GUNGAKU

CONFUCIAN BUSHIDO
REDEFINING SAMURAI
ETHICS IN PEACE
JUKYO

WANG YANG MING
YOMEIGAKU
(INTERNAL)

NEO-CONFUCIAN
SHUSHIGAKU
(EXTERNAL)

HAGAKURE BUSHIDO
(DEATH FRENZY, THE WAY
OF THE WARRIOR IS FOUND
IN DYING)

KOKUGAKU BUSHIDO
"NATIVE STUDIES" AND
REDEFINING JAPAN, SHINTO

BUDO SHOSHINSHU BUSHIDO
(DIE IN YOUR FUTON...)

MEIJI BUSHIDO
NATIONAL IDENTITY, LOYALTY
TO EMPEROR, POPULAR AND
STATE NATIONALISM,
"SAMURAIZATION" OF
JAPANESE PEOPLE

"CHRISTIAN" BUSHIDO
NITOBE INAZO, UCHIMURA KANZO,
JOHN IMAI TOSHIMICHI ETC.
INTERNATIONAL

SHOWA BUSHIDO
ULTRANATIONALISM, MILITA-
RISM, IMPERIALISM, ECO-
NOMIC SUCCESS

HEISEI BUSHIDO
JAPANESE IDENTITY, MORALITY
IDEALS BASED ON TRADITION,
CULTURAL NATIONALISM

What is Bushido?

Popularly known in Japan and now in the West as the "Way of the warrior," Bushido was an ethical code followed by the Samurai heroes of feudal Japan. Many people harbor romantic images of swashbuckling Samurai willingly putting themselves in great danger to fight for a just cause. Living their life on a knife edge, Samurai would ultimately meet their death with a serene smile. Staunchly loyal and honorable men, they embraced physical and mental suffering in their quest to train body and mind.

While this prevailing but somewhat exaggerated image of the indomitable Samurai spirit has enduring appeal, it is too simplistic. All countries have a tendency to glorify their warrior past and proudly embellish its heroic elements as representing the very fiber of their national psyche. Japan is no different. However, much of what has been written about the Samurai, making them out to be superhuman crackerjacks of justice, is pure fiction. This is not to say that the image we have today of fearless Samurai is not entirely without substance. Far from it!

The history of Samurai thought, purportedly built on an apparent contempt for life, provides a genuine doorway into the deepest reaches of the human condition. It is the vestiges of Samurai philosophy and culture that attract millions of people around the world to the Japanese martial arts, not just as competitive sports or for the learning of self-defense, but to access a profound source of timeless wisdom that aspires to self-perfection and peace of mind.

This wisdom is real and is still relevant. To understand its relevance, however, one has to put aside sentimentalized notions of the omnipotent Samurai hero and think of Samurai simply as another group of people struggling to navigate the complexities of the society in which they lived.

Back to the initial question, what is Bushido? There is and can be no single definition. The term itself was one of many for warrior ethics and was, in fact, rarely used until later in the age of the Samurai. Even if Bushido is defined broadly as the "Samurai way of life," the huge disparity in warrior ideology and behavior in different eras, regions, political regimes, and even among Samurai of various ranks, cannot be ignored. Nevertheless, for the sake of simplicity, I will use the term Bushido throughout this book.

Generally speaking, warrior ideals in Japan developed in three distinct phases:

1. The warrior ethos before the Edo period (pre-1600), an ideology forged in an environment of constant warfare. (The reader should note, however, that the term "Bushido" did not as yet exist!)

2. The intellectual Bushido developed mainly by Confucian and military scholars during the Edo period (1603–1868), an extended time of relative peace when the warrior spirit was refocused on self-cultivation to maintain social order.

3. The modern repackaging of Bushido in the Meiji period (1868–1912) and beyond. This phase represents a dramatic reinterpretation of Samurai culture in the formulation of a new Japanese national identity. To this day, many Japanese people associate Bushido with Japanese-ness and as the source of their most noble national traits.

An examination of the most emblematic texts from each period shows how the "Way of the warrior" was constantly evolving. For example, "war histories" from around the early medieval Kamakura (1185–1333) and Muromachi (1336–1573) periods, such as *The Tale of the Heike* and the *Taiheiki*, portray an ideal centered on faithfulness to one's lord and reckless abandon in battle. This was indeed the "ideal," which means that the "reality" was a very different story. In real terms, early medieval allegiance was honed by economic considerations. Samurai actively and selfishly pursued their own interests in a "you scratch my back and I'll scratch yours" type of contractual fealty, a relationship of mutual benefit referred to as *go'on to hoko* (reward for service).

On the other hand, later medieval texts such as the *Koyo-gunkan*, written around the end of the 16th century when Japan was emerging from a century and a half of constant civil war, provide a window into the Samurai psyche at a time when treachery and disloyalty were an ever-present reality.

Typically glorifying the history of the clan they were written about, these commentaries offer practical advice to ensure survival in times of pandemonium. Compared to the earlier literature, the demands on Samurai of the 16th century meant that the content was more pragmatic and often scornful of enemies and irresponsible clansmen. Part propaganda and part reproach, the chronicles are fine examples of historical revisionism. As such, the reliability of the content is questionable. Reading between the lines, however, the true value of the texts is found in realistic insights into the anxieties faced by these professional men-at-arms and their struggle to prevail.

Once peace and stability enveloped Japan during the Edo period, warrior thought matured into sophisticated "articles of faith" incorporating Confucian and Taoist ideals of social order and governance as well as Buddhist appreciation of the ephemeral world championing the aesthetic of death.

Representative works from this period include Miyamoto Musashi's *Gorin-no-sho* (Book of Five Rings) and Yagyu Munenori's *Heiho Kadensho*. Both were written by master swordsmen in the early Edo period and both testify to how the art of war could be applied to all aspects of life in addition to fighting.

The orderly climate of the mid to later Edo period (18th and early 19th centuries) nurtured clearly defined ethical codes for a "tamed" Samurai class. This was a golden age for Samurai ideology, which drew on shared experiences of the past mixed with "new age" considerations to help redefine the warrior *raison d'être* in a time of peace.

Loyalty to the point of death and other idioms of Samurai honor endured but were demonstrated through impeccable behavior in daily life rather than in the thick of battle. After all, there were no more battles to be involved in. The prominent scholar and strategist Yamaga Soko, for example, lectured that to justify the privileged existence of the Samurai in an era when he no longer needed to fight, their duty was to provide moral leadership. In fact, as recipients of stipends, Samurai lived off the backs of those who toiled in the fields. The function of a warrior in a peaceful society, Soko argued, was to be a role model for the common people by fulfilling their duty and willingness to protect those who grew the food they ate.

Selfless dedication to service was also the main message in Yamamoto Jocho's classic book, *Hagakure* (1716). Jocho (aka Tsunetomo) declared that the role of Samurai of the Nabeshima clan was to fortify resolve to sacrifice their lives for the greater good of the domain and for the lord. One achieved this, according to Jocho, by "living as if already dead."

One of Jocho's contemporaries, Daidoji Yuzan, wrote another Bushido classic, *Budo Shoshinshu* (ca. 1725). His work weaves indigenous Shinto and Confucian ideals into a "how to be a Samurai" compendium outlining appropriate behavior for all warriors irrespective of clan affiliation. He underscored strict adherence to protocol as an indicator of honor and mindfulness of death to avoid conflict altogether.

Although the Meiji Restoration (1868) and the subsequent dismantling of Tokugawa social structures led to the eventual annulment of the Samurai class, this did not mean the end of Bushido. From the mid-1880s, especially after the Sino-Japanese War (1894–95), a new interpretation of Bushido emerged that served as a powerful emotive force in the process of modernization and the creation of a national identity. Ironically, perhaps, it is from this time that Bushido became a more commonly used term in Japan.

Like many other countries, Japan became engulfed in a wave of popular and state nationalism in the late 19th century. What made the Japanese distinct? This was the question on Japanese minds as they constructed a common identity *vis-à-vis* the rest of the world.

With the *Conscription Ordinance* of 1872, young men from all backgrounds were obliged to undergo three years of military service, an occupation that not so long ago was reserved for Samurai only. Conscripts were indoctrinated in a modern military code of honor specified in *The Imperial Rescript to Soldiers and Sailors* (1882). Although no mention is made of Bushido, its portrayal of the "ideal soldier" draws on values such as "loyalty," "propriety," and "frugality," all key words in past Bushido treatises. The code demanded absolute loyalty to the emperor and gallant service to the nation. Soldiers were encouraged to see themselves as the modern incarnation of Samurai.

Memorized verbatim in the nation's schools, documents such as *The Imperial Rescript on Education* (1890) implored Japanese children to "Render illustrious the best traditions of your forefathers." Samurai culture provided a treasure trove of symbolism in the conception of "Japanese-ness." Bushido was thus disseminated by scholars and educators as nothing less than the indomitable spiritual pulse of the nation.

Following the publication of the Quaker Nitobe Inazo's *Bushido: The Soul of Japan* (1900), Bushido came to be known and disseminated beyond Japan's shores. Originally written in English, Nitobe set out to convince the West that although Christianity had yet to become established in Japan, the traditional principles of Bushido had imbued all Japanese with a sense of morality and mode of decorum that were not inferior. In fact, he argued, Bushido and Christianity were highly compatible.

Born into a Samurai family several years before the Meiji Restoration of 1868, Nitobe's modern reinterpretation of Bushido has become arguably the most influential explanation, providing a blueprint for its popular understanding today.

With so many variants over so many centuries, how do we make sense of the enigmatic Samurai mind throughout history? It is not easy to synthesize the myriad concepts which defined their existence. This book provides a new approach to understanding the subtleties of Bushido. The chapters are organized to provide a clear overview of the evolution of Samurai culture.

A picture says a thousand words. Visual thinking and graphical ways of presenting ideas and information are often a helpful way to convey complex ideas. The technique I use in this book is a kind of "concept mapping" in which the relationships between key concepts and ideas are illustrated. Readers will be able to see how the ideas and more abstract aspects of Bushido are connected.

I have successfully utilized this visual method of teaching for many years at my university in Japan. This book is based on my lecture materials. I find that diagrams are invaluable for conveying the complexities of Samurai culture to Japanese and non-Japanese students alike. Diagrams help transcend linguistic barriers and enable students to grasp perplexing content with their eyes, not just their ears as they listen to the passionate ramblings of their professor.* I am grateful to my good friend Baptiste Tavernier who did a wonderful job of turning my multimedia slides into most of the aesthetically pleasing illustrations you see in this book.

The fundamental principle of the Samurai mind was affirmation of the beauty of life, a fact that is routinely obscured by the contradictions inherent in their world. Breaking through the superfluous and often paradoxical information regarding this fascinating subject, I wrote this book as a frame of reference and hope that it provides clues into how Samurai wisdom is still in many ways pertinent in the 21st century.

---

* Most of the diagrams that I created in this book are the result of my doodling as I tried to make sense of how the various episodes in Japanese history and Bushido fit together. The ones on the following pages, however, were modeled largely or loosely from the following books—p. 11: M. Takemitsu, *Nihonjin Nara Shitte Okitai Bushido* (2011), 53; p. 15: M. Takemitsu, *Mikka de Wakaru Nihonshi* (2010), 43; p. 16: Takemitsu (2010), 79; p. 29: Takemitsu (2010), 121; p. 30 Takemitsu (2010), 123, 125; p. 127: R. Mori, *Bushido ga Yoku Wakaru* (2010), 123; p. 32: Takemitsu (2010) p. 137; p. 33: Takemitsu (2010), 135; p. 34: Takemitsu (2010), 147; p. 35: Takemitsu (2010), 155; p. 36: Takemitsu (2010), 157; p. 41: A. Kawai, *Hayawakari Nihonshi* (1997), 231; p. 53: R. Ikegami, *Zukai Sengoku Busho* (2010), 61; p. 77: H. Yamamoto, *Nihonjin no Kokoro Bushido Nyumon* (2014), loc 465 of 1,902; p. 108: Yamamoto (2014), loc 1,295 of 1,902; p. 120: Kishi Y. Kaku K., *Zukai Zatsugaku Bushido* (2007), 175; p. 125, Yamamoto (2014), loc 1,397 of 1,902; p. 145: Mori (2010), 71; p. 147: Mori (2010), 73; p. 149: Mori (2010), 87; p. 150, Mori (2007), 71; p. 151, Mori (2007), 85; p. 151: Discover Japan, *Bijinesu ni Ikasu Bushido no Oshie* (2013), 55; p. 151: Mori (2007), 85; p. 154: Mori (2010), 45.

Overview of Japanese History

ca. 4000 BC	**Jomon Culture** – Prehistoric culture.
ca. 300 BC	Yayoi Culture – Agricultural society based on wet-rice (*inasaku*) cultivation. Metal implements.
ca. AD 300	**Tomb Period (250–538) and Asuka Period (538–710)** Colossal burial mounds (*kofun*) and clay terracotta statuettes (*haniwa*) reveal the appearance of influential clans.
AD 552	**Introduction of Buddhism into Japan**
AD 645	**Taika Reforms** – Political and economic reforms based on the Chinese model of governance. Conscription army.
710–794	**Nara Period** – Founding of the first capital in Nara (Heijo). Increasing influence of Buddhist temples. New military systems introduced that encouraged privatization.
794–1185	**Heian Period** – Burgeoning of aristocratic culture (literature, court ceremony, etc.) in the new capital Heian-kyo (Kyoto). Proliferation of private estates.
1185–1333	**Kamakura Period** – Commencement of military rule with the formation of the first shogunate in Kamakura. Imperial government continues in Kyoto together with the shogunate in the east of Japan. Warrior authority begins to supersede nobles.
1333–36	**Kenmu Restoration** – Attempt by Emperor Go-Daigo to restore direct imperial rule following the decline of the Kamakura shogunate.
1336–1573	**Ashikaga (Muromachi) Period** – A new warrior government is established in Kyoto. Increasing sophistication of warrior culture with widespread patronage of the arts.
1467–1568	**Warring States Period (Sengoku)** – Prolonged civil war between rival warlords (*daimyo*) starting with the Onin War (1467–77) until Oda Nobunaga entered Kyoto in 1568.
1568–1600	**Azuchi Momoyama Period** – Gradual national unification through the rise of powerful warlords Oda Nobunaga, Toyotomi Hideyoshi, and Tokugawa Ieyasu.
1600–1867	**Tokugawa (Edo) Period** – Japan unified under the Tokugawa shogunate in Edo (present-day Tokyo). Peace lasts for 250 years, providing an environment for significant economic and artistic advances. Golden years for the development of samurai ideals.
1868–1912	**Meiji Period** – Restoration of imperial power, dismantling of class distinctions, and the establishment of a modern nation state with the widescale introduction of legal, military, educational, and social conventions from the West.
1912–26	Taisho Period
1926–89	Showa Period
1989–2019	Heisei Period

Military and economic world power.

Chapter 1
Historical Overview

"**B**ushido" literally means the "Way (*do*) of the warrior (*bushi*)." Most people in the West are more familiar with the alternative term "*Samurai*," which derives from the Japanese verb *saburau*, meaning "to serve." The terms are now used interchangeably and refer to hereditary professional warriors who wielded political power in medieval and early modern Japan. As professional warriors, Samurai differed from peasant conscript soldiers in both the ancient and modern periods. As hereditary warriors, their existence also differed from officials who were assigned military duty in ancient times, and also from the modern career soldier. Coming from aristocratic roots, how and when did Samurai eclipse the nobles, their original masters, to become the dominant political leaders of Japan?

Samurai Beginnings

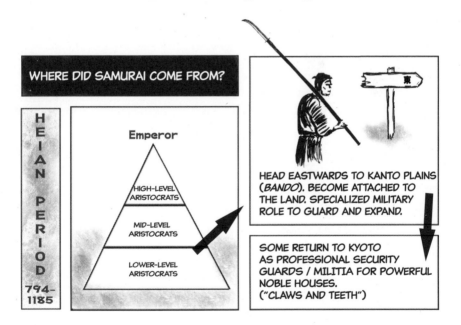

WHERE DID SAMURAI COME FROM?

HEIAN PERIOD 794–1185

Emperor

HIGH-LEVEL ARISTOCRATS

MID-LEVEL ARISTOCRATS

LOWER-LEVEL ARISTOCRATS

HEAD EASTWARDS TO KANTO PLAINS (*BANDO*). BECOME ATTACHED TO THE LAND. SPECIALIZED MILITARY ROLE TO GUARD AND EXPAND.

SOME RETURN TO KYOTO AS PROFESSIONAL SECURITY GUARDS / MILITIA FOR POWERFUL NOBLE HOUSES. ("CLAWS AND TEETH")

There is no easy answer to this question as many factors were involved. In simple terms, however, the gradual rise of Samurai to political prominence was prompted by the court abolishing its conscript army in the 8th century under which service was forced on unwilling peasants and led by inexperienced nobles. Seen as unacceptably burdensome, each household with three or more adult males was required to send one of them for military training for up to three years, and even had to provide him with equipment. In its stead, the court government conjured up various systems in which the military became privatized and was made the domain of provincial magnates and mid- to low-level nobles.

These ad hoc military experts formed networks and competed for wealth and influence as security guards or private armies for noble factions in the capital and provinces. The profession provided useful opportunities for advancement among the middle- to lower-ranked aristocrats. Martial ability was their ticket to a successful career in a mutually beneficial arrangement with the powerful families who controlled the seat of government. To this end, many headed to the Kanto plains in the east and areas far from the capital to develop and protect estates and entered into armed alliances with local elites.

A strong *esprit de corps* was forged between these men-of-arms through shared combat experience, giving rise to a subculture based on violence that was distinct from the central nobles. To the Samurai, honor gleaned through a show of valor superceded all else. Honor was worth dying for.

To maintain their privileges and monopoly on government posts, upper-level nobles in Kyoto employed experts for their own private armies. The court itself actively recruited mercenaries to bolster its military and policing system.

With the onset of the Kamakura period (1185–1333), Samurai became mainstream political players. Minamoto-no-Yoritomo created Japan's first warrior government (Bakufu) in 1192 in the little seaside town of Kamakura, located near present-day Tokyo. Yoritomo's Bakufu by no means replaced the Kyoto-based court government. In fact, he needed validation from the emperor and was conferred by him the official title Sei'i Tai-Shogun ("barbarian quelling generalissimo").

The Bakufu was a "warrior union" of sorts in which Yoritomo occupied the top position and monopolized lines of communication with the court government. Although the Bakufu is called a military government, it was in essence a ministry for homeland security that coexisted with the central imperial government.

The mindset of the Kamakura-period warrior was centered on loyalty underpinned by a spirit of autonomy. They were tough men who found meaning in the rough-and-ready lifestyle of the frontier lands. An honorable reputation was earned through ability in combat. It was only a matter of time before nobles capitulated in the face of their unbridled political aspirations that emerged in the 12th to 14th centuries. Let us now look at events leading to the formation of the Bakufu in Kamakura in more detail, and how warrior hegemony became established for the next seven centuries.

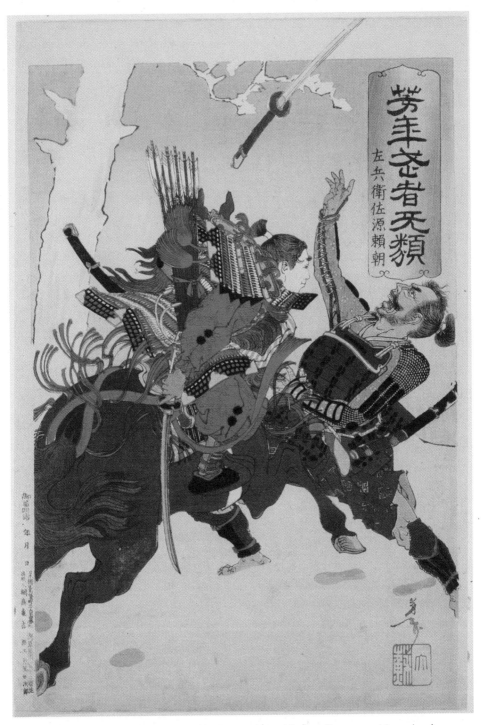

Sahyōenosuke Minamoto no Yoritomo Attacking an Enemy on Horseback.
(Los Angeles County Museum of Art)

1. No Picnic in the Provinces

Rise of the "Strong Men"

THE NUMBER OF *BUSHIDAN* INCREASED FROM THE HEIAN THROUGH TO THE KAMAKURA PERIODS...

PEASANTS RECRUITED TO FARM WARRIORS HONE THEIR FIGHTING SKILLS

LANDOWNERS ARGUE OVER TERRITORIAL BOUNDARIES, WATER ETC...

BIG FIGHTS ERUPT!! ALLIED GROUPS BAND TOGETHER...

"STRONG MEN" PREVAIL!!

RISE OF MILITARY ELITES AND PRIVATE ARMIES

From around the 10th century, public (*kokuga*) and private estates (*shoen*) in the provinces increased in size and number. The typical estate was organized like a pyramid, with the farmers at the base. Above them were the estate managers (low- to mid-level aristocrats), central proprietors (temples, shrines, or central nobles in Kyoto), and the guarantor (high-level government official who received tax payoffs).

Wealthy courtiers and religious institutions purchased land, developed more land, and were not averse to forcefully taking land belonging to others if the opportunity presented itself. Arguments over control of rivers for irrigation, boundary disputes, and rebellions were not uncommon. Simple quarrels sometimes erupted into full-scale conflicts in which relatives and allied groups were called in to assist. The theater of battle amplified the influence of those who performed with distinction, and landowners enlisted mercenaries ("strong men") for protection.

Gang Warfare

With no standing army of its own, the court's control of the provinces went into decline in the latter part of the Heian period as *shoen* became independent of central administration. Local landowners and the low- to mid-level aristocrats dispatched to the provinces to oversee estates became attached to the land, took control of the local administrative bodies, and solidified alliances with related families. These leagues were known as *bushidan*, or "bands of military men," and they steadily spread throughout Japan.

The original *bushidan*, formed around the 10th century, were mainly family groups that could be mobilized for specific campaigns to protect holdings or to settle disputes with rival groups. The bands gradually extended their membership by absorbing unrelated fighting men into their paternalistic hierarchical organizational structure.

Genesis of Supreme Warrior Chieftains

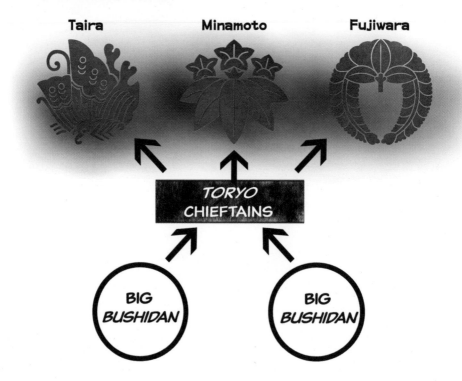

Overall leadership of the expanding bands of professional warriors was eventually consolidated by men who descended from offshoots of the imperial family. In particular, the noble houses of the Taira (aka Heike or Heishi), the Minamoto (aka Genji), and the Fujiwara came to control vast landholdings and commanded the allegiance of sizeable *bushidan* as *toryo*, or "supreme chieftains."

With powerful noble families in court controlling massive private armies, jostling for position and power was inevitable, and by the middle of the 12th century factionalism was going to plunge Japan into absolute turmoil.

Two insurgencies fought in the capital of Kyoto led to the ascendancy of warrior domination on the political scene: the Hogen Disturbance in 1156 followed by the Heiji Disturbance in 1160. Be warned. The events were a tangled web of intrigue and treachery that are hard to comprehend, but are particularly relevant in that they set the country up for Samurai rule.

4. The Hogen Disturbance (1156)

Power Struggles in Court

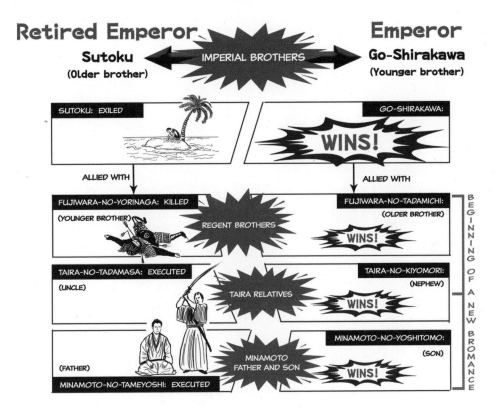

Following the death of Emperor Toba in 1156, the first year of the Hogen era, rivalries in court erupted into a violent clash involving the Taira, Minamoto, and Fujiwara families in what is known as the Hogen Disturbance (1156). The newly installed emperor, Go-Shirakawa, was supported by Fujiwara-no-Tadamichi (1097–1164). His brother Yorinaga (1120–56) decided to support the retired Emperor Sutoku (Go-Shirakawa's older brother), who wanted his son to be the emperor. Sutoku also had the backing of Minamoto-no-Tameyoshi (1096–1156), but Tameyoshi's son Yoshitomo joined Taira-no-Kiyomori in support of Go-Shirakawa. Sutoku's followers tried in vain to wrest power from the other faction but Yorinaga was killed, Tameyoshi was executed, and Sutoku was sent into exile. Go-Shirakawa was the victor, but real power in court ended up in the hands of his supporters.

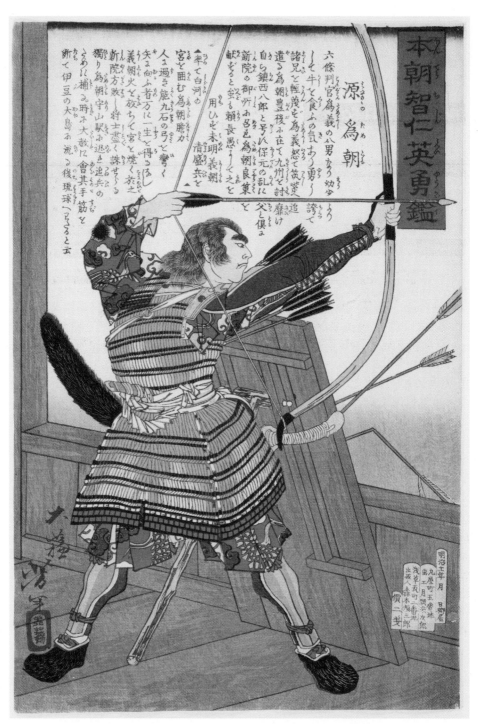

Minamoto no Tametomo with a Bow. (Los Angeles County Museum of Art)

5. The Heiji Disturbance (1160)

Court Struggles Part 2

HOWEVER, IN 1160...

Emperor Nijo (Go-Shirakawa's son)

SPOILS GO TO KIYOMORI AND MICHINORI

FUJIWARA-NO-NOBUYORI: KILLED

JEALOUSY...
RETAINER CLASH

FUJIWARA-NO-MICHINORI: KILLED

MINAMOTO-NO-YOSHITOMO: KILLED

JEALOUSY...
GENPEI CLASH
(MINAMOTO VS. TAIRA)

TAIRA-NO-KIYOMORI:

LAST MAN STANDING.
WINNER TAKES ALL!!

Although they were allies in the Hogen Disturbance, Yoshitomo and Kiyomori fought against each other four years later, during the Heiji Disturbance of January 1160 (Heiji 1). Kiyomori had been the beneficiary of greater rewards than his colleagues. He held considerable influence in court, together with Fujiwara-no-Michinori, through their sway over the now retired Emperor Go-Shirakawa. When Kiyomori was absent from Kyoto on pilgrimage, a disgruntled Yoshitomo joined forces with Fujiwara-no-Nobuyori (1133–60) and placed Go-Shirakawa under arrest. Michinori was killed before Kiyomori could return to quell the revolt. Go-Shirakawa's son, Emperor Nijo (1143–65), was taken into protective custody by Kiyomori when he returned, and Yoshitomo and Nobuyori were summarily killed as rebels. This essentially removed Minamoto and Fujiwara influence from court and gave the Taira family under Kiyomori the freedom to rule unopposed. Yoshitomo had three infant sons—Minamoto-no-Yoritomo, Noriyori, and Yoshitsune—whom Kiyomori exiled instead of having them killed. This act of mercy was to come back to haunt him.

6. The Genpei War (1180–85)

The Final Showdown

DAN NO URA
THE FINAL BATTLE

Kiyomori became the Grand Minister of State, and in 1180 he enthroned his infant grandson as Emperor Antoku. His despotic behavior in court earned him many enemies. Prince Mochihito (1151–80), the second son of retired Emperor Go-Shirakawa, was furious at having been passed over twice for succession to the throne. He sought the support of the last remaining Minamoto in court, Yorimasa, and together they revolted. Both were killed by Kiyomori in battle but the fuse had been lit for an all-out campaign to rid the court of Taira influence. The exiled son of Yoshitomo, Yoritomo, rallied his Minamoto kin and other enemies of the Taira residing mainly in the east of Japan and sounded the drums of war.

Yoritomo established his base in Kamakura, and after amassing around 200,000 warriors commanded by his younger brother Yoshitsune, pushed the Taira westward over the course of the next five years. The final battle was a naval encounter in Dannoura in 1185. The infant emperor, Antoku, drowned when his grandmother, Kiyomori's wife Tokiko, held onto him and jumped into the ocean with her servants in a tragic act of mass suicide. The Taira were finished.

Minamoto warrior Kajiwara Genda Kagesue fighting during the Genpei War.
(Wikimedia Commons)

Kamakura Shogunate

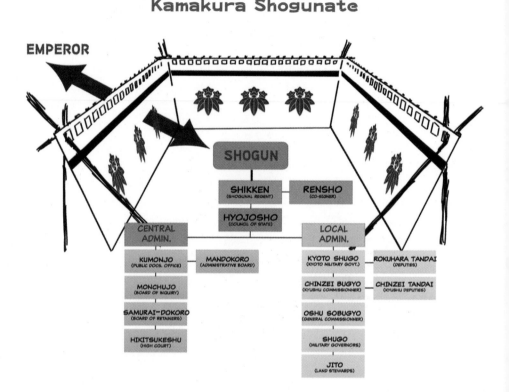

After the Genpei War and the vanquishing of the Taira nobles, the influence of the Minamoto and their allies blossomed with the formation of the Kamakura Bakufu (tent government) by Yoritomo. In 1192, Yoritomo was bestowed the title of Sei'i Tai-Shogun ("barbarian quelling generalissimo") by the emperor. This is the year that many scholars traditionally recognize as the establishment of the Kamakura Bakufu, but Yoritomo had, in fact, begun to gradually set up his governmental apparatus from 1180. Yoritomo's initiatives included legally elevating loyal vassals to the status of privileged "housemen" (*gokenin*), who showed loyalty only to him. After 1185, he rewarded vassals with the titles and accompanying land rights of governor (*shugo*) and land steward (*jito*) to keep them happy and loyal.

In this "master–servant" arrangement, Yoritomo guaranteed his vassals proprietorship of their ancestral lands and allotted bonus territories to repay them for their allegiance. These vassals, who also had their own vassals, were to serve their master in a pact that was mutually beneficial.

For all intents and purposes, the system of fealty established by Yoritomo resembled a kind of war-based pyramid scheme, with the peasants toiling in the ricefields at the bottom and Samurai in the battlefields competing for position and power.

It is important to note, however, that the creation of the Bakufu did not spell the end of court authority. The imperial capital of Japan remained in Kyoto and the military capital became Kamakura. It did, however, signify the beginning of new conventions and rules that instilled distinctive sentiments of Samurai self-identity.

8. Kamakura's Decline

Minamoto supremacy did not last long after Yoritomo's death. In reality, it was the Hojo clan that ruled for more than a century until they also met their demise with the Kenmu Restoration (1333). The Hojo family was a scion of Taira-no-Tokiie. His grandson, Hojo Tokimasa (1138–1215), befriended Yoritomo who ended up marrying his daughter Hojo Masako (1157–1225). Tokimasa and Masako took control of the shogunate from 1203. As regents to the figurehead shoguns after Yoritomo, the Hojo became the de facto military rulers.

The Hojo were relatively effective governors for a while and formulated the first warrior legal code called the *Goseibai Shikimoku* (1232), which solidified warrior rule further and weakened court influence through creating legal constraints.

The third regent, Hojo Tokimune (r. 1268–84), successfully defended Japan against two attempted Mongol invasions in 1274 and 1281. Japan was, in fact, saved more by the weather. Two typhoons decimated the Mongol fleets before they could finish what they started. This good fortune for the Japanese proved to be a double-edged sword as the men mobilized for the task were not compensated adequately for their service. (An invading force bring boots but no booty.)

Eventually, dissatisfaction grew among the Bakufu's vassals. The bonds of allegiance that kept the government intact started to crumble and the Kamakura shogunate was doomed in 1333 when Emperor Go-Daigo instigated the Kenmu Restoration.

Go-Daigo ascended the throne in 1318, a time of great instability for the Kamakura shogunate, a fact that was not lost on him. Go-Daigo decided to unseat the "eastern barbarians" once and for all and restore imperial power. His plot was discovered in 1324 and he was sent into exile but continued with his subversive plans upon his return to Kyoto in 1333. The shogunate sent generals Ashikaga Takauji and Nitta Yoshisada to punish him but they changed allegiance to Go-Daigo and the Kamakura government was no more.

Rise and Fall of the Hojo Regents

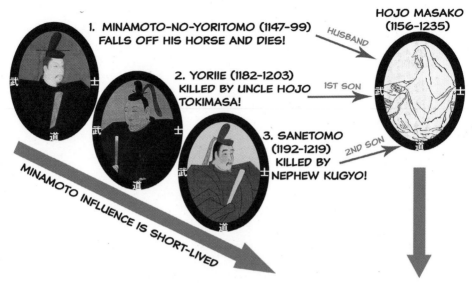

1. MINAMOTO-NO-YORITOMO (1147-99) FALLS OFF HIS HORSE AND DIES!

HUSBAND

HOJO MASAKO (1156-1235)

2. YORIIE (1182-1203) KILLED BY UNCLE HOJO TOKIMASA!

1ST SON

3. SANETOMO (1192-1219) KILLED BY NEPHEW KUGYO!

2ND SON

MINAMOTO INFLUENCE IS SHORT-LIVED

Power passes to the Hojo family (Regents)
Shogun ⇨ Figurehead

MONGOL INVASIONS
1274 = 40,000 MEN
1281 = 140,000 MEN

GOSEIBAI SHIKIMOKU (1232)
CONCEPT OF *DORI* = REASON

TYPHOONS ⇨ MONGOL DEFEAT ⇨ PRESTIGE FOR HOJO (SHORT-LIVED!)

KUBLAI KHAN

SHOGUNATE CAN'T KEEP PROMISE OF LOOT FOR WARRIOR SERVICE. PRIESTS ALSO SOUGHT REWARDS FOR THE POWER OF PRAYER (DIVINE WIND)

GROWING DISSATISFACTION WITH HOJO REGENCY

- 1333 - ASHIKAGA TAKAUJI SENT TO PUNISH RETIRED EMPEROR GO-DAIGO FOR REBELLING
- TAKAUJI CHOOSES TO SUPPORT GO-DAIGO (KENMU RESTORATION)
- NITTA YOSHISADA SENT TO PUNISH TAKAUJI AND *GO-DAIGO*
- YOSHISADA ALSO TURNS AGAINST THE SHOGUNATE
- HOJO TAKATOKI (14TH HOJO REGENT) COMMITS SUICIDE

Kamakura Shogunate Overthrown
Mantle of Warrior Power Transfers to Kyoto

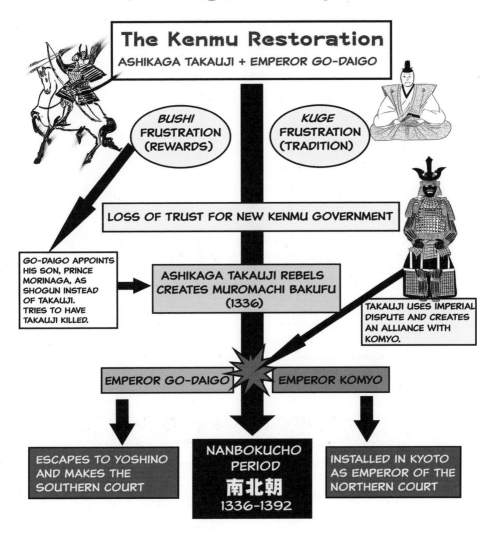

The Kenmu Restoration
ASHIKAGA TAKAUJI + EMPEROR GO-DAIGO

BUSHI FRUSTRATION (REWARDS)

KUGE FRUSTRATION (TRADITION)

LOSS OF TRUST FOR NEW KENMU GOVERNMENT

GO-DAIGO APPOINTS HIS SON, PRINCE MORINAGA, AS SHOGUN INSTEAD OF TAKAUJI. TRIES TO HAVE TAKAUJI KILLED.

ASHIKAGA TAKAUJI REBELS CREATES MUROMACHI BAKUFU (1336)

TAKAUJI USES IMPERIAL DISPUTE AND CREATES AN ALLIANCE WITH KOMYO.

EMPEROR GO-DAIGO

EMPEROR KOMYO

ESCAPES TO YOSHINO AND MAKES THE SOUTHERN COURT

NANBOKUCHO PERIOD
南北朝
1336-1392

INSTALLED IN KYOTO AS EMPEROR OF THE NORTHERN COURT

Takauji coveted the title of shogun, but Go-Daigo, distrustful of Takauji's aspirations, refused to bestow it upon him. The court then ordered Nitta Yoshisada to attack his rival Takauji because of differing views on how to govern the country. Takauji won and the newly formed Kenmu government disintegrated.

Having bet on the wrong horse, Go-Daigo was forced to flee from Kyoto to Yoshino after Takauji installed Komyo as the new emperor. This gave Takauji the chance to establish the Muromachi (aka Ashikaga) Bakufu in Kyoto. The series of events also led to another struggle that pitted Go-Daigo's Southern (Yoshino) Court against the Ashikaga-supported Northern Court in Kyoto. This is known as the Nanbokucho period, or the age of the Southern and Northern Courts.

Muromachi Bakufu

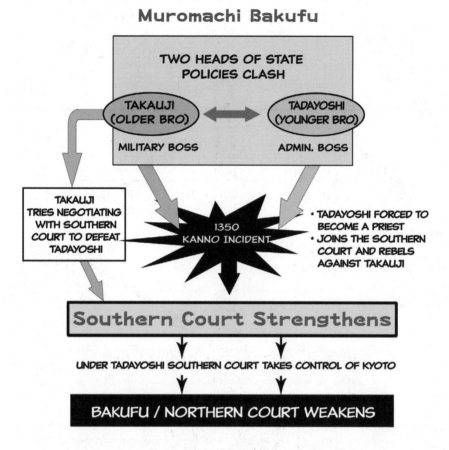

TWO HEADS OF STATE POLICIES CLASH

TAKAUJI (OLDER BRO) ⟷ TADAYOSHI (YOUNGER BRO)

MILITARY BOSS   ADMIN. BOSS

TAKAUJI TRIES NEGOTIATING WITH SOUTHERN COURT TO DEFEAT TADAYOSHI

1350 KANNO INCIDENT

- TADAYOSHI FORCED TO BECOME A PRIEST
- JOINS THE SOUTHERN COURT AND REBELS AGAINST TAKAUJI

Southern Court Strengthens

UNDER TADAYOSHI SOUTHERN COURT TAKES CONTROL OF KYOTO

BAKUFU / NORTHERN COURT WEAKENS

Takauji prevails, Tadayoshi poisoned. Bakufu comes under single authority.

Although Takauji assumed the mantle of power as shogun, his ability to govern was lacking and his brother Tadayoshi effectively ruled for him for a decade. Their tenuous relationship was shattered with the Kanno Incident. This was sparked when Takauji made Ko-no-Moronao his deputy, a move that irked Tadayoshi. Tadayoshi tried unsuccessfully to depose Moronao, eventually deciding that killing him was the only solution. His plan failed and in 1349 Tadayoshi was forced out of the government and into the priesthood.

In 1350, Tadayoshi rebelled against his brother by joining forces with the Southern Court. Emperor Go-Murakami made Tadayoshi the general of his army and he defeated Takauji in 1351. Takauji got revenge the following year at the Battle of Suruga Sattayama. Although the brothers managed to reconcile

Amakasu Ômi no Kami from the series *A Hundred Generals Brave in Battle at Kawanakajima*. (Wikimedia Commons)

their differences, it was a brief reprieve. Tadayoshi took flight to Kamakura with Takauji's army in hot pursuit. They reconciled again but Tadayoshi suddenly died in custody in March 1352. The war chronicle *Taiheiki* suggests that Tadayoshi was poisoned.

Samurai culture became increasingly sophisticated during the Muromachi period (1333–1568). An honorable reputation through combat prowess was tempered by a new appreciation for the arts and a burgeoning sense of aestheticism that was as urbane as the court protocols after which it was modeled. With the influence of the court completely diminished, the Samurai were well equipped militarily and culturally to take the reins of power once and for all. But things were never going to be easy for this second and weakest of the three shogunates.

10. The Squabbling Continues

To expand authority into the provinces, Ashikaga shoguns were compelled to recognize the position and authority of military governors who oversaw them. Toward the end of the 14th century, *shugo daimyo*, as they were known, wielded substantial power and autonomy. The shogunate did not command a central army of its own and relied on the patronage of these independently powerful lords. Before long, the balance of power tilted in their favor, largely due to ineffectual rule and infighting between ambitious shogunate vassals.

Matters came to a head in the mid-1460s. Shogun Ashikaga Yoshimasa and his wife Hino Tomiko were unable to produce an heir. Yoshimasa wished to step down and asked his brother Yoshimi to give up his life as a priest and take over the office in 1464. Not long after, Tomiko gave birth to a boy, Yoshihisa (1465–89), and demanded that he be made the next shogun. This family tiff sparked the ten-year Onin War from 1467. Hosokawa Katsumoto, the shogunal deputy, supported Yoshimi and Yamana Sozen, Katsumoto's father-in-law and powerful *shugo daimyo*, threw his weight behind Yoshihisa. Other clans quickly jumped on the war wagon, joining sides with ulterior motives of settling their own family disputes.

Although the succession dispute was resolved before long, the fighting continued until 1477 and left Kyoto in a state of ruin. The shogunate continued until 1573 but it was ineffectual and the country plummeted into over a century of civil war, known as the Warring States (Sengoku) period.

A New Era of Domestic Chaos

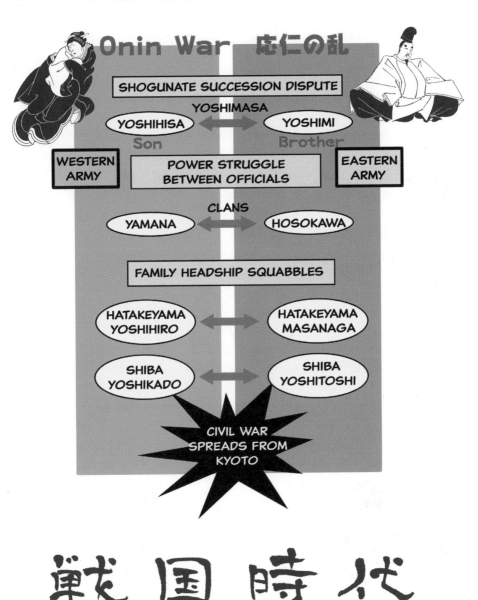

Onin War 応仁の乱

SHOGUNATE SUCCESSION DISPUTE

YOSHIMASA

YOSHIHISA ⟷ YOSHIMI

Son   Brother

| WESTERN ARMY | POWER STRUGGLE BETWEEN OFFICIALS | EASTERN ARMY |

CLANS

YAMANA ⟷ HOSOKAWA

FAMILY HEADSHIP SQUABBLES

HATAKEYAMA YOSHIHIRO ⟷ HATAKEYAMA MASANAGA

SHIBA YOSHIKADO ⟷ SHIBA YOSHITOSHI

CIVIL WAR SPREADS FROM KYOTO

戦 国 時 代

Massive Power Shift

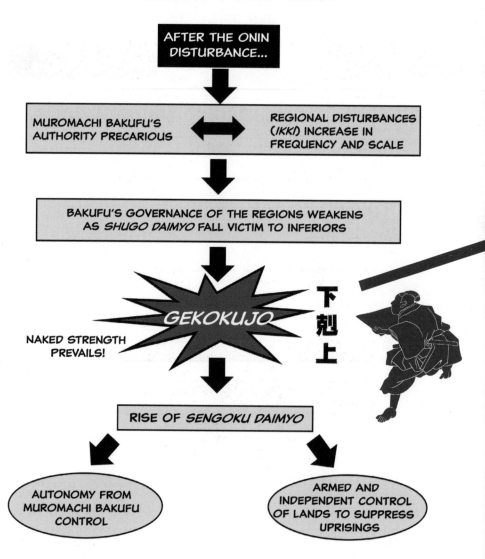

AFTER THE ONIN DISTURBANCE...

MUROMACHI BAKUFU'S AUTHORITY PRECARIOUS ⟷ REGIONAL DISTURBANCES (*IKKI*) INCREASE IN FREQUENCY AND SCALE

BAKUFU'S GOVERNANCE OF THE REGIONS WEAKENS AS *SHUGO DAIMYO* FALL VICTIM TO INFERIORS

GEKOKUJO 下剋上

NAKED STRENGTH PREVAILS!

RISE OF *SENGOKU DAIMYO*

AUTONOMY FROM MUROMACHI BAKUFU CONTROL

ARMED AND INDEPENDENT CONTROL OF LANDS TO SUPPRESS UPRISINGS

The chaotic political environment was a golden time for opportunists. A well-known phenomenon of the era was *gekokujo*, whereby persons of inferior status displaced their superiors in bold-faced mutiny. So much for loyalty! A passage in the *Taiheiki*, the mid-14th century war tale, describes the age of *gekokujo* vividly: "Now is a time when vassal kills lord and child kills father. Only naked strength prevails. Indeed, it is the extremity of *gekokujo*."

The Rise of Sengoku Warlords

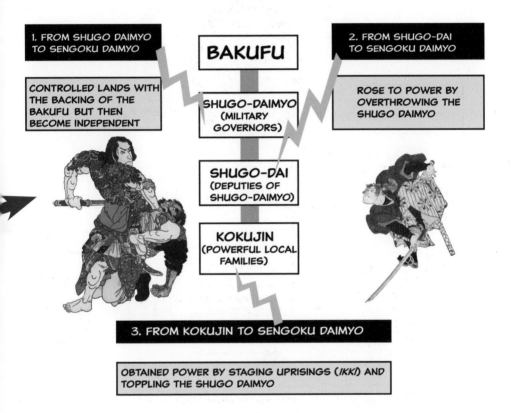

1. FROM SHUGO DAIMYO TO SENGOKU DAIMYO

CONTROLLED LANDS WITH THE BACKING OF THE BAKUFU BUT THEN BECOME INDEPENDENT

BAKUFU

SHUGO-DAIMYO (MILITARY GOVERNORS)

SHUGO-DAI (DEPUTIES OF SHUGO-DAIMYO)

KOKUJIN (POWERFUL LOCAL FAMILIES)

2. FROM SHUGO-DAI TO SENGOKU DAIMYO

ROSE TO POWER BY OVERTHROWING THE SHUGO DAIMYO

3. FROM KOKUJIN TO SENGOKU DAIMYO

OBTAINED POWER BY STAGING UPRISINGS (*IKKI*) AND TOPPLING THE SHUGO DAIMYO

Shugo daimyo were provincial military governors appointed by the Muromachi Bakufu. They became semi-autonomous governors over one or more provinces. To keep their power in check, the shogunate required *shugo daimyo* in central Japan to reside in Kyoto. This gave rise to the need for deputies (*shugo-dai*), tasked with managing provincial matters in the absence of their *shugo daimyo*.

After the Onin War, the country was in such disarray that many *shugo daimyo* were toppled by provincial proprietors known as *kokujin*, or even their own deputies. The vanquishers established themselves as a new style of voraciously ambitious, independent warlords called *sengoku daimyo*.

By the 1540s, *sengoku daimyo* controlled all the provinces but were locked in war as they fought tooth and nail to increase their landholdings. From the 1570s to 1600, the so-called "Three Great Unifiers," Oda Nobunaga, Toyotomi Hideyoshi, and Tokugawa Ieyasu, finally succeeded in subduing all of them.

Oda Nobunaga (1534–82)

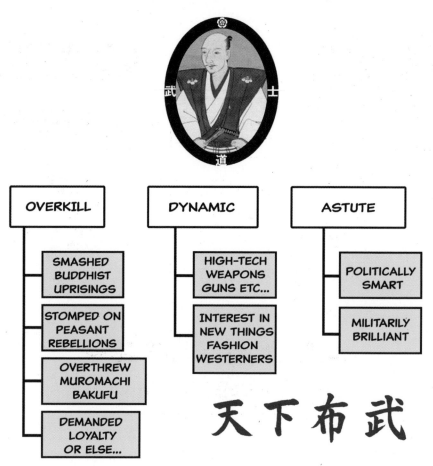

Nobunaga inherited his father's territories at the age of seventeen and rapidly rose to be *the* alpha *sengoku daimyo*. He is credited with transforming the way war was waged in Japan. Fascinated by European culture, weapons, and new inventions, it was his adoption of superior military technology that set him apart from others. Nobunaga's seal, *Tenka Fubu* ("cover that which is under the sky with the sword"), perfectly describes his aspirations.

Nobunaga is remembered for his brutal suppression of any and all who refused to yield to his demands. He slaughtered his way to rule over twenty provinces. He armed his men with firearms, thereby displacing traditional mounted archers as the predominant force in battle. He also constructed iron-plated naval vessels of the likes never before seen in Japan.

Creation of Semi-Professional Warriors

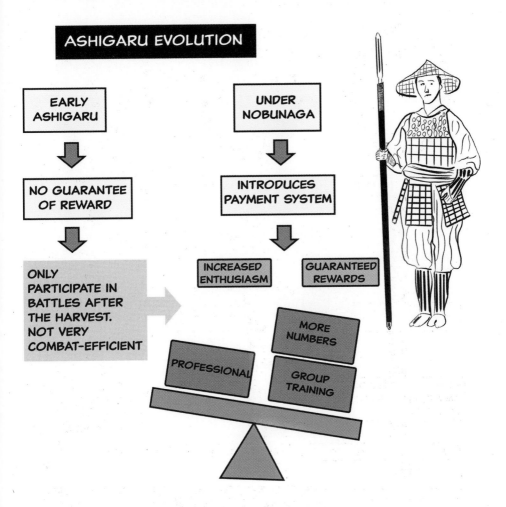

ASHIGARU EVOLUTION

EARLY ASHIGARU

↓

NO GUARANTEE OF REWARD

↓

ONLY PARTICIPATE IN BATTLES AFTER THE HARVEST. NOT VERY COMBAT-EFFICIENT

UNDER NOBUNAGA

↓

INTRODUCES PAYMENT SYSTEM

↓

INCREASED ENTHUSIASM

GUARANTEED REWARDS

PROFESSIONAL

MORE NUMBERS

GROUP TRAINING

In terms of tactics, Nobunaga trained his peasant foot soldiers in large-scale regimental maneuvers, dressed them in distinctive "team" uniforms, and even paid them so that war could be waged as a year-long sport rather than a seasonal affair between harvests.

Of his many military campaigns, the notorious 1571 Siege of Mount Hiei was a one-sided bloodbath in which he led 30,000 men to raze around 400 temples on the sacred mountain of Mount Hiei and its surrounds. The uncooperative Tendai monks of Mount Hiei were a constant thorn in Nobunaga's side, so he mercilessly killed thousands of them and their peasant parishioners to keep them in check.

Given the acrimony he invited as he made his way to the top, it is hardly surprising that he was destined to meet a grizzly end.

Nobunaga's Fall, Hideyoshi's Rise

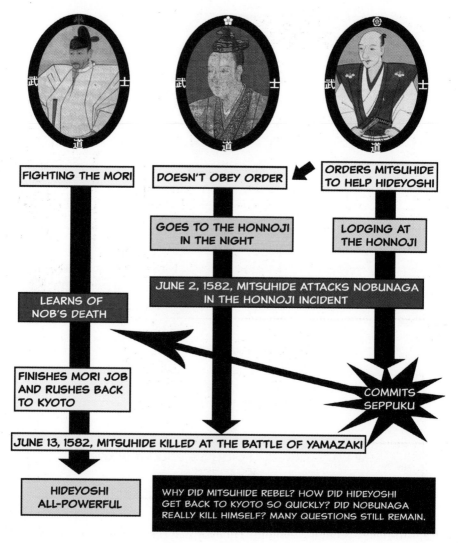

FIGHTING THE MORI · **DOESN'T OBEY ORDER** · **ORDERS MITSUHIDE TO HELP HIDEYOSHI**

GOES TO THE HONNOJI IN THE NIGHT · **LODGING AT THE HONNOJI**

LEARNS OF NOB'S DEATH

JUNE 2, 1582, MITSUHIDE ATTACKS NOBUNAGA IN THE HONNOJI INCIDENT

FINISHES MORI JOB AND RUSHES BACK TO KYOTO · **COMMITS SEPPUKU**

JUNE 13, 1582, MITSUHIDE KILLED AT THE BATTLE OF YAMAZAKI

HIDEYOSHI ALL-POWERFUL

WHY DID MITSUHIDE REBEL? HOW DID HIDEYOSHI GET BACK TO KYOTO SO QUICKLY? DID NOBUNAGA REALLY KILL HIMSELF? MANY QUESTIONS STILL REMAIN.

In 1582, Nobunaga's right-hand man, Toyotomi Hideyoshi, was on the verge of taking a Mori clan stronghold. Being one of the last thorns needing to be plucked from Nobunaga's thick skin, he departed for the siege from his castle in Azuchi and stopped off at the Honnoji Temple for a ceremonial cup of tea. Somewhat vulnerable without his usual entourage, one of his "trusted" commanders, Akechi Mitsuhide, turned on his master for reasons that still remain a mystery. Mitsuhide burned the temple and Nobunaga was forced to commit suicide. It was a classic example of medieval treachery, but Mitsuhide did not live long enough to capitalize on it. Hideyoshi saw to that.

Toyotomi Hideyoshi (1537-98)

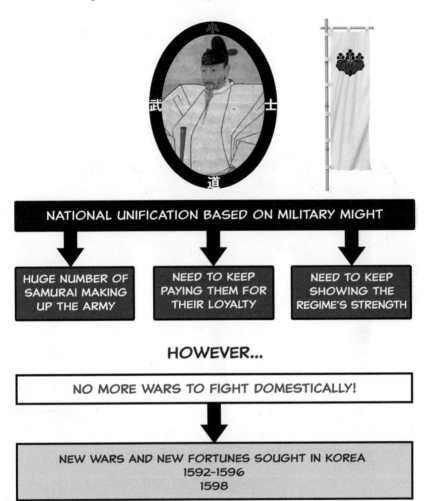

NATIONAL UNIFICATION BASED ON MILITARY MIGHT

- HUGE NUMBER OF SAMURAI MAKING UP THE ARMY
- NEED TO KEEP PAYING THEM FOR THEIR LOYALTY
- NEED TO KEEP SHOWING THE REGIME'S STRENGTH

HOWEVER...

NO MORE WARS TO FIGHT DOMESTICALLY!

NEW WARS AND NEW FORTUNES SOUGHT IN KOREA
1592-1596
1598

Rags-to-riches general Toyotomi Hideyoshi succeeded his lord, Oda Nobunaga, and managed to subjugate the *sengoku daimyo*, thus bringing the Warring States period to an end. His many directives were to have a lasting effect on Japanese society. For example, he decreed that only Samurai could carry weapons. He further tightened class distinctions by requiring all Samurai to cease farming and take up residence in castle towns.

He also conducted an extensive national land survey to instigate an orderly tax system, and marked out domain boundaries, thereby restricting freedom of travel. He ordered two invasions of Korea between 1592 and 1598, perhaps to legitimize his position and mitigate the danger of rebellion by the massive number of now redundant Samurai (*ronin*) roaming the land.

Hideyoshi's Fall, Ieyasu's Rise

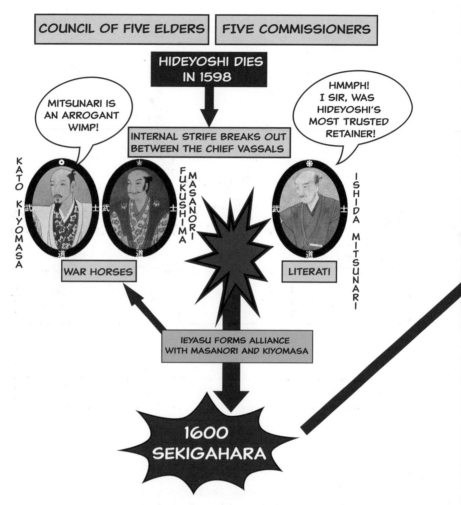

Not being of noble birth, Hideyoshi could not attain the title of shogun and opted instead for the post of Imperial Regent. On his deathbed in 1598, he formed the Council of Five Elders and Five Commissioners from among his most trusted generals to ensure that his infant son Hideyori would succeed him as heir when Hideyori came of age.

Mitsunari was appointed as one of the commissioners to oversee the business of the realm. Many believed it was not due to his martial ability but more to his skill in the tea ceremony! Mitsunari suspected Tokugawa Ieyasu of abusing his position in the council to usurp Toyotomi authority. After the death of another member of the council, Maeda Toshiie, Ieyasu became supreme in terms of seniority, causing factional tensions to mount.

The Battle of Sekigahara

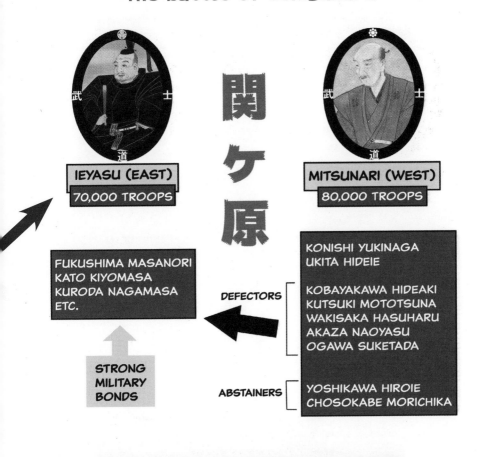

関ヶ原

IEYASU (EAST)
70,000 TROOPS

MITSUNARI (WEST)
80,000 TROOPS

FUKUSHIMA MASANORI
KATO KIYOMASA
KURODA NAGAMASA
ETC.

KONISHI YUKINAGA
UKITA HIDEIE

KOBAYAKAWA HIDEAKI
KUTSUKI MOTOTSUNA
WAKISAKA HASUHARU
AKAZA NAOYASU
OGAWA SUKETADA

DEFECTORS

STRONG
MILITARY
BONDS

ABSTAINERS

YOSHIKAWA HIROIE
CHOSOKABE MORICHIKA

THE BATTLE OF SEKIGAHARA RESULTED IN A
RESOUNDING VICTORY FOR THE EASTERN ARMY

The council began to fall apart when Mitsunari increased his hostility and spread rumors about Ieyasu's designs to take Hideyori's birthright. Two of Hideyoshi's top generals, Kato Kiyomasa and Fukushima Masanori, despised Ishida Mitsunari for his aloofness and sided with Ieyasu when he made his move.

In the disorder that resulted and the scramble to recruit supporters and quell opposition, Ishida Mitsunari seized the initiative and created a coalition army to challenge Ieyasu and his allies. Mitsunari arranged his army on the western side of Sekigahara. He planned to engage Ieyasu's eastern army in the center of the valley, providing an opportunity for Kobayakawa Hideaki to attack from the left flank. At the pivotal point in the battle, Mitsunari's allies defected and the western army was trounced.

The End of the Toyotomi Clan

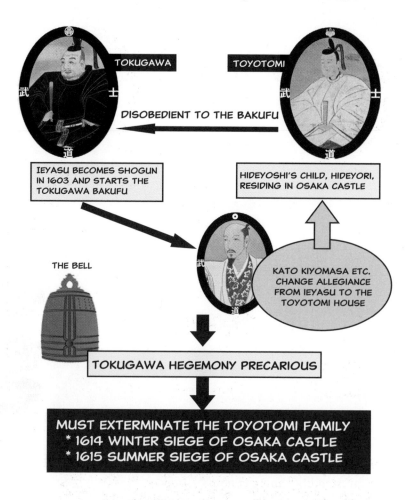

TOKUGAWA

TOYOTOMI

DISOBEDIENT TO THE BAKUFU

IEYASU BECOMES SHOGUN IN 1603 AND STARTS THE TOKUGAWA BAKUFU

HIDEYOSHI'S CHILD, HIDEYORI, RESIDING IN OSAKA CASTLE

THE BELL

KATO KIYOMASA ETC. CHANGE ALLEGIANCE FROM IEYASU TO THE TOYOTOMI HOUSE

TOKUGAWA HEGEMONY PRECARIOUS

MUST EXTERMINATE THE TOYOTOMI FAMILY
* 1614 WINTER SIEGE OF OSAKA CASTLE
* 1615 SUMMER SIEGE OF OSAKA CASTLE

After Sekigahara, Ieyasu reallocated land to his allies, and on March 24, 1603 he was bestowed the title of shogun by the emperor. Although only a *daimyo* now, the last threat to his regime was Toyotomi Hideyori. Samurai who harbored ill-feeling towards Ieyasu united around Hideyori as the "rightful ruler." Ieyasu fabricated an excuse to punish Hideyori by finding fault with an inscription on a bell cast for a Toyotomi-sponsored temple. Ieyasu claimed that it contained a code praying for the ruin of him and the Tokugawa clan.

Toyotomi supporters were ordered to leave Osaka Castle. When they refused, Tokugawa forces attacked on two occasions in the "Winter Siege" and the "Summer Siege." Osaka Castle fell late in 1615 and most of those inside, including Hideyori, were put to the sword. With the Toyotomi line extinguished, Tokugawa authority was now absolute.

13. Order at Last

Tokugawa Period Society

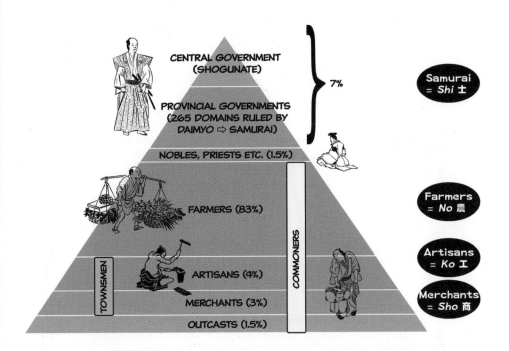

Edo Population Approx. 3 Million

CENTRAL GOVERNMENT (SHOGUNATE)

PROVINCIAL GOVERNMENTS (265 DOMAINS RULED BY DAIMYO ⇨ SAMURAI)

7%

NOBLES, PRIESTS ETC. (1.5%)

FARMERS (83%)

ARTISANS (4%)

MERCHANTS (3%)

OUTCASTS (1.5%)

TOWNSMEN

COMMONERS

Samurai = Shi 士

Farmers = No 農

Artisans = Ko 工

Merchants = Sho 商

The Tokugawa period (aka Edo period, 1603–1868) was a time of relative calm, political stability, and economic growth. Semi-autonomous domains known as *han* were answerable to the Tokugawa shogunate, which served as the central authority based in Edo. Those who supported Ieyasu before Sekigahara were given special dispensation as *fudai daimyo* while those who opposed him, but were spared, became *tozama daimyo* and were treated with suspicion thereafter.

The government distinguished four classes: Samurai, farmers, artisans, and merchants. Distinctions were often hazy, and apart from the Samurai at the top other groups were not superior to each other. Concerned with possible rebellion, the shogunate forced *daimyo* to reside part of the time in Edo and leave their family members as hostages when they returned. Also wary of foreign influences, the shogunate banned Christianity and strictly forbade international travel and trade.

The shogunate in Edo had its own elite in-house vassals called *hatamoto* (bannermen), but the majority of Samurai served in hierarchically structured domains which were all answerable to the shogun.

Samurai Hierarchy

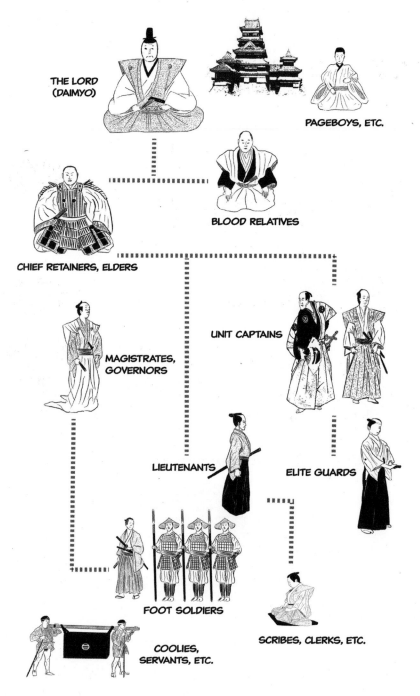

THE LORD (DAIMYO)

PAGEBOYS, ETC.

BLOOD RELATIVES

CHIEF RETAINERS, ELDERS

MAGISTRATES, GOVERNORS

UNIT CAPTAINS

LIEUTENANTS

ELITE GUARDS

FOOT SOLDIERS

SCRIBES, CLERKS, ETC.

COOLIES, SERVANTS, ETC.

HIGH-LEVEL   MID-LEVEL   LOW-LEVEL

Tradition Versus Modernization

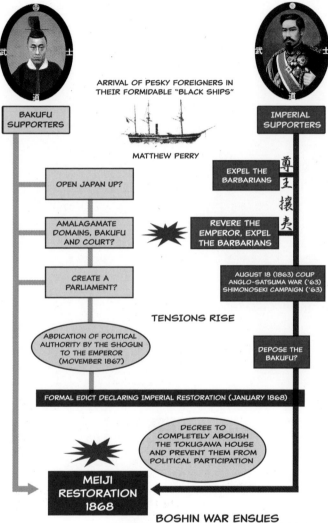

ARRIVAL OF PESKY FOREIGNERS IN THEIR FORMIDABLE "BLACK SHIPS"

MATTHEW PERRY

BAKUFU SUPPORTERS

IMPERIAL SUPPORTERS

OPEN JAPAN UP?

EXPEL THE BARBARIANS

AMALAGAMATE DOMAINS, BAKUFU AND COURT?

REVERE THE EMPEROR, EXPEL THE BARBARIANS

CREATE A PARLIAMENT?

AUGUST 18 (1863) COUP
ANGLO-SATSUMA WAR ('63)
SHIMONOSEKI CAMPAIGN ('63)

TENSIONS RISE

ABDICATION OF POLITICAL AUTHORITY BY THE SHOGUN TO THE EMPEROR (MOVEMBER 1867)

DEPOSE THE BAKUFU?

FORMAL EDICT DECLARING IMPERIAL RESTORATION (JANUARY 1868)

DECREE TO COMPLETELY ABOLISH THE TOKUGAWA HOUSE AND PREVENT THEM FROM POLITICAL PARTICIPATION

MEIJI RESTORATION 1868

BOSHIN WAR ENSUES
IMPERIAL LOYALISTS LED BY CHOSHU, SATSUMA, AND TOSA DOMAINS ROUT SHOGUNATE FORCES

The Tokugawa period was an immensely prosperous time for merchants who supplied the military class. They became wealthier than the bureaucratized Samurai themselves whose main source of income was a fixed stipend based on rank and tied to agricultural production. Stipends failed to keep up with other sectors of the economy, and forbidden from engaging in commercial activities many Samurai lived in relative poverty.

In its last thirty years in power, the Tokugawa regime was beset by peasant uprisings, Samurai discontent, and fiscal difficulties. Moreover, the mounting menace of Western intrusion sparked a movement for the restoration of imperial rule to unify and modernize the country. When Commodore Matthew Perry from the United States visited Japan's waters with his squadron of "Black Ships" in 1853 to seek, or force, trade relations, the time was ripe for anti-shogunate forces to build momentum and mobilize.

The Satsuma and Choshu domains laid the foundation for a monumental social revolution. The last shogun, Tokugawa Yoshinobu (1837–1913), came under mounting pressure due to his weak response to the Western threat, and the Tosa domain recommended that he abdicate in favor of imperial governance. Towards the end of 1867, Yoshinobu tentatively agreed to these proposals for change. However, on January 1, 1868, the Satsuma forces forced the process by surrounding the palace in Kyoto and announcing the restoration of imperial rule. Yoshinobu sent his forces from Edo to engage the imperialists at the Battle of Toba-Fushimi in what became the first confrontation of the Boshin War (1868–69).

Changing of the Guard

BOSHIN WAR 1868-69

HAKODATE

BATTLE OF HAKODATE
MAY, 1869

AIZU

BATTLE OF NAGAOKA CASTLE
MAY–JULY, 1868

NAGAOKA

BATTLE OF AIZU
AUG.–SEPT., 1868

CHOSHU KYOTO

EDO

BATTLE OF UENO
MAY 15, 1868

TOSA

BATTLE OF TOBA FUSHIMI
JAN. 1, 1868

SATSUMA

Following the Meiji Restoration in 1868, domains were abolished in favor of a prefectural system headed by governors selected by the central government. Furthermore, in 1869, class distinctions of *shi-no-ko-sho* (warrior, farmer, artisan, merchant) were replaced with *kazoku* (nobles), *shizoku* (former Samurai), and *heimin* (commoners). Thus, with the formation of the Meiji government, Samurai symbolism and privileges were removed incrementally, and bureaucratic and military positions were open to men by virtue of their ability rather than hereditary status. With the *danpatsu-rei* edict of 1871, *shizoku* cut off their now passé topknots (*mage*) and were not required to carry swords. Following the *Conscription Ordinance* of 1873, all men over the age of twenty were obligated to complete three years of military training. When the *Sword Ban Order* (*haito-rei*) of 1876 was issued, *shizoku* were forbidden to carry swords in their sashes. This right was instead transferred to military officers and policemen, whose ranks constituted a mix of class backgrounds.

Shizoku received special stipends from the government from 1873 as a kind of severance pay, but they were forced to exchange these for government bonds in 1876, leading to the impoverishment of many. Although a significant number of *shizoku* were able to re-establish themselves in government services, education, and private enterprise, there were still those who remained destitute with no tangible skills suited to modern commerce or their rapidly changing circumstances.

The period between 1874 and 1877 was far from tranquil. More than thirty rebellions were started by disenfranchised former warriors. The biggest and last uprising against the Meiji government was the Satsuma Rebellion led by the former imperial stalwart, Saigo Takamori of Satsuma. Commanded by Okubo Toshimichi, Saigo's former friend, also from Satsuma, the government marshaled over 65,000 men and fought for eight months to suppress Saigo's rebels. Saigo committed suicide on September 24, 1877, and the Samurai counter-revolution finally came to an end the following year with the assassination of Okubo.

15. In Summary

Samurai of the Ages

	Kamakura	Muromachi	Tokugawa
GOVERNMENT	SEMI-CENTRAL WARRIOR GOVERNMENT (BAKUFU) BASED IN KAMAKURA	BAKUFU MOVES TO KYOTO. PROVINCIAL WARLORDS VIE FOR SUPREMACY	PACIFICATION AND CONSOLIDATION. PROVINCIAL DOMAINS ANSWERABLE TO EDO BAKUFU
RELATIONSHIP WITH LORD	GO'ON HOKO (FAVOR & SERVICE) RELATIVE AUTONOMY	HIERARCHICAL WITH HIGH EXITS IF BETTER OFFERS FOUND ELSEWHERE	HIERARCHICAL AND HEREDITARY WITH LOW EXITS
MILITARY	MAN-TO-MAN COMBAT BETWEEN MOUNTED WARRIORS IN PRIVATE ARMIES	ADVANCES IN TECHNOLOGY AND ORGANIZATION FACILITATE LARGE SCALE BATTLES	MILITARY FUNCTION OF SAMURAI MAINTAINED THROUGH MARTIAL ARTS BUT NO WARS TO FIGHT
HONOR	CENTERED ON INDIVIDUAL MILITARY PROWESS AND AUTONOMY. VALOR AND FEATS IN BATTLE	MILITARY PROWESS AND FEATS IN BATTLE BUT BALANCED WITH ABILITY IN REFINED ARTS	MILITARY PROWESS IS REPLACED BY DISCIPLINED COMPORTMENT IN DAILY LIFE
POPULATION	3%–5%	5%–7%	5%–7%
WARRIOR'S WAY TERMS	TSUWAMONO-NO-MICHI YUMIYA TORU MI-NO-NARAI BANDO MUSHA-NO-NARA MUSHA-NO-NARAI TSUNE-NO-NARAI KYUSETSU-NO-MICHI KYUBA-NO-MICHI YUMIYA-NO-MICHI...	KYUBADO MUSHADO BUHEN-NO-MICHI OTOKO-NO-MICHI SAMURAIDO TODO...	HEIHO-NO-MICHI BUKYO BUJI BU-NO-MICHI SHI (SAMURAI)-NO-MICHI SHIDO (SAMURAI-DO) BUSHI-NO-MICHI BUDO BUSHIDO...

Chapter 2
The Profession of Arms
戦闘士の生活

If the splendid descriptions of Samurai exploits in the classical war tales are to be believed, warfare in medieval Japan was a gentlemanly sport, even though it was quite gory. Celebrated chronicles such as the *Heike Monogatari* and the *Taiheiki,* with their accounts of battle rituals, tragic heroes, and unrestrained bravery in the struggles of the just over the unjust, stirred the blood of generations of Samurai.

A Samurai would not hesitate to sacrifice his life in battle if cornered or in defense. He could be trusted not to surrender meekly as the enemy targeted his position, and he believed that posthumous benefits would be bestowed upon him and his descendants for valor. His motivation to die in battle is commonly misconstrued as signifying unbreakable bonds of loyalty between an overlord and his followers. Pledges of loyalty were indeed crucial to the warrior code. Nevertheless, there was a calculated side to this service contract and medieval warriors would readily change allegiance if conditions appeared to be better elsewhere. Such fickle fidelity changed in the Tokugawa period when serfdom in a particular domain was hereditary and withdrawing from such positions was uncommon. However, in the Warring States period and the tumultuous times before it, service was very much a deadly game of musical chairs.

Whatever the situation, the warrior was *ideally* obligated to repay his lord's special favor (*go'on*) with service (*hoko*). This meant participation in military campaigns and an expectation that he would fight valiantly to the bitter end, if need be. Battle was a stage for the warrior to demonstrate his mettle. Recognized gallantry and a collection of trophy heads, preferably of well-known enemy warriors, would be handsomely rewarded. If killed in the throes of combat, his death would be viewed as that of a hero. He could rest in peace assured that his lord would continue granting favor to his progeny, or at least his good family name would have survived for another generation.

In other words, even in death the benefit gained from heroic courage was the "currency of honor," a legacy that would be inherited by his sons and grandsons. His magnificence in battle would be recounted as family lore and the fortune of his household or clan would endure. Conversely, cowardice was the emperor of all maladies that would be a perpetual stain on the family's reputation.

The Way of the warrior was born of armed conflict in which combat ability was paramount. Even in times of peace, war was never far from the Samurai's mind. Every mundane ritual or custom in his daily life could be traced back to preparation for the "big day"—death and honor in battle.

With the onset of the Tokugawa period, war became a distant memory. Samurai read the old narratives and imagined what battle was really like. They fantasized about it and daydreamed of how, if given the opportunity, they too would exit this ephemeral world in a blaze of glory. In this way, the realities of war were romanticized by future Samurai who had never experienced mortal combat. An acceptance of mortality remained at the core of their culture, to the extent that a "beautiful self-willed death" was virtually yearned for. They were like martyrs without a cause.

To appreciate the warrior ideal throughout history, it helps to have at least a cursory understanding of Samurai combat, its rites, culture, tools, and philosophy.

1. Rituals of War

Early Medieval Warfare

* ONE-ON-ONE COMBAT
* MOUNTED WARRIORS IN PRIVATE ARMIES
* HONOR BASED ON PRIDE IN MILITARY SKILL AND AUTONOMY

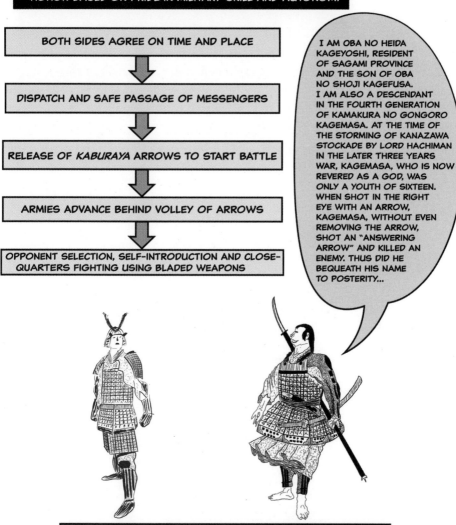

BOTH SIDES AGREE ON TIME AND PLACE

DISPATCH AND SAFE PASSAGE OF MESSENGERS

RELEASE OF *KABURAYA* ARROWS TO START BATTLE

ARMIES ADVANCE BEHIND VOLLEY OF ARROWS

OPPONENT SELECTION, SELF-INTRODUCTION AND CLOSE-QUARTERS FIGHTING USING BLADED WEAPONS

I AM OBA NO HEIDA KAGEYOSHI, RESIDENT OF SAGAMI PROVINCE AND THE SON OF OBA NO SHOJI KAGEFUSA. I AM ALSO A DESCENDANT IN THE FOURTH GENERATION OF KAMAKURA NO GONGORO KAGEMASA. AT THE TIME OF THE STORMING OF KANAZAWA STOCKADE BY LORD HACHIMAN IN THE LATER THREE YEARS WAR, KAGEMASA, WHO IS NOW REVERED AS A GOD, WAS ONLY A YOUTH OF SIXTEEN. WHEN SHOT IN THE RIGHT EYE WITH AN ARROW, KAGEMASA, WITHOUT EVEN REMOVING THE ARROW, SHOT AN "ANSWERING ARROW" AND KILLED AN ENEMY. THUS DID HE BEQUEATH HIS NAME TO POSTERITY...

ARE THERE ANY AMONG YOU WHO ARE WORTHY OF FIGHTING SUCH AN ILLUSTRIOUS DUDE AS I?

Battle scenes in Samurai literature are described as conforming to a defined order: both sides agree on the time and place; messengers return to their armies as they face off; turnip-head arrows are released to signal the commencement of hostilities; armies advance shooting arrows as they go; when close quarters are reached, self-introductions are blurted out so that suitable opponents can be identified, and fighting begins with bladed weapons; the safety of non-combatants is guaranteed.

Showmanship was an important feature, with individual warriors seeking duels from horseback or on foot with champions of the enemy force. But let us assume that there was considerable poetic license here, especially with the self-introductions!

As much as it is appealing to emphasize the chivalrous manner in which war was conducted, the reality was often quite different. That is not to say, however, that no special rituals were involved. The Samurai were a superstitious bunch and certain rules were followed. But when it mattered, winning was everything and method was of little consequence. If devious means were required to triumph, then so be it.

One does not need to look far in historical sources to find proof of what can only be labeled less than gentlemanly behavior. If attacking the enemy front on seemed a suicidal task, it was considered smarter to assault hidden weaknesses instead, maybe at night, in an ambush, or by secretly convincing the enemy's allies to defect at an inconvenient moment. Anything was permissible for the sake of victory.

Augmentation of Firepower

INCREASE OF MOBILIZED MANPOWER

- PEASANTS DRAFTED INTO ARMIES OF REGIONAL LORDS
- PIKES (LONG POINTY SPEARS THAT DIDN'T REQUIRE MUCH TRAINING)

INDIVIDUAL FIGHTS --> REGIMENTED STRATEGIES

- "LOOK AT ME, AREN'T I FABULOUS?" APPROACH RESTRICTED
- BIGGER FORCES REQUIRED DISCIPLINE TO ENACT BATTLE TACTICS
- INCREASED IMPORTANCE OF FOOT SOLDIERS (*ASHIGARU*)

CONSTRUCTION OF CASTLES

- PERMANENT STRONGHOLDS BUILT IN STRATEGIC LOCATIONS

INTRODUCTION OF FIREARMS

- INTRODUCTION OF FIREARMS RAISED THE PROMINENCE OF SWORDS?
- WARRIORS SOUGHT CLOSE-QUARTER ENGAGEMENTS QUICKER
- LESS ROOM TO MOVE DUE TO LARGER NUMBERS

Later medieval warfare was conducted on a much larger scale than previously. Certain rules for engagement still applied, but there was little room for showmanship when giant Warring States armies clashed.

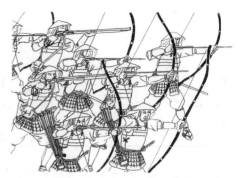

Following the introduction of firearms, especially from the mid to late 16th century, warriors tried to close the distance as quickly as possible to engage at close quarters. Musket balls could penetrate even the sturdiest armor, so lighter and less cumbersome suits became fashionable. Some scholars believe that firearms replaced bows in battle but, in fact, the two weapons would often be used in tandem to great effect.

"Shock and awe" was the name of the game now, but warrior cultural idiosyncracies endured in various forms.

The Big Day

Let us look at what was involved leading up to a fight. Technology and the scale of battle changed over the centuries but the rituals of war remained.

The time and place of a battle was heavily influenced by the *daimyo*'s military advisor who used divination to determine the best strategy. Once decided, warriors participated in a special ceremony called *sankon no gi* in which abalone (*uchi-awabi*), dried chest-

"Sankon no gi." Reproduced in Sasama, *Nihon Gassen Zuten.*

nut (*kachi-guri*), and kelp (*kombu*) were consumed. This was a play on words: *uchi* means "to strike" [the enemy], *kachi* is "to triumph," and *yoro-ko[m]bu* is "to rejoice" in the victory. After praying to the deities, the troops would leave their encampment with the battle cry "EI EI" (by the general) followed by a resounding "OOOOooo!" by the men.

Battles would start with the release of a *kaburaya*, an arrow that whistled as it flew, much like the starting hooter for a game of football.

Even though teamwork, in particular discipline and cohesion, in the ranks was crucial for victory, "individual play" remained an important element. A Samurai needed to have his feats recognized, and there were specific acts of valor that were worth dying for. Suicidal though it was, the most acclaimed feat was being the first to charge headlong into the enemy forces.

"The Ichiban Yari charge." Reproduced in Sasama, *Nihon Gassen Zuten*.

Strategy in Large Scale Confrontations

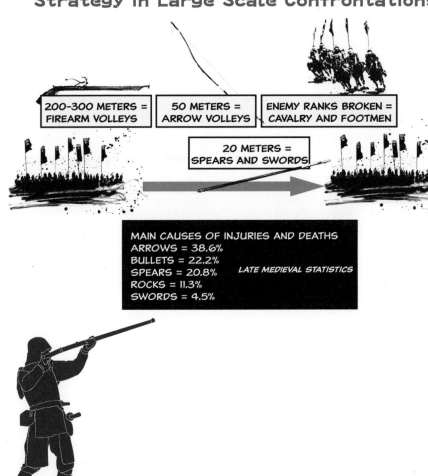

| 200-300 METERS = FIREARM VOLLEYS | 50 METERS = ARROW VOLLEYS | ENEMY RANKS BROKEN = CAVALRY AND FOOTMEN |

20 METERS = SPEARS AND SWORDS

MAIN CAUSES OF INJURIES AND DEATHS
ARROWS = 38.6%
BULLETS = 22.2%
SPEARS = 20.8%   *LATE MEDIEVAL STATISTICS*
ROCKS = 11.3%
SWORDS = 4.5%

Prize Giving

After the battle, an official would set up his post to record all relevant data, including the number of casualties, the causes of death or injury, brave deeds worthy of commendation, and the grisly head count. Samurai would take the heads of warriors they had felled or appropriated in other ways and have them cleaned and groomed by the womenfolk ready for presentation.

Not all heads were the same. The higher ranked the warrior, the more a head was worth. The head of a general, or the first head taken in the encounter, were coveted prizes and competition for recognition of this honor was fierce. The official would be sure to seek witness testament to corroborate any claims. Even the direction in which the dead man's eyes were gazing was considered either auspicious or not and changed the value of the trophy.

If the warrior was too busy fighting for his life to stoop down and remove heads, or if he had too many victims on the end of his sword to carry back, he would take the noses instead, preferably with the moustaches still attached to prove that his victim was a genuine warrior and not a boy or woman.

A ceremony in which the general inspected the heads was then performed. It was carried out in accordance with strict procedures and with armed guards standing by in case the ghosts of the fallen sought revenge.

The gruesome custom of arranging heads to claim prizes.
Reproduced in Sasama, *Nihon Gassen Zuten*.

The Spoils of War

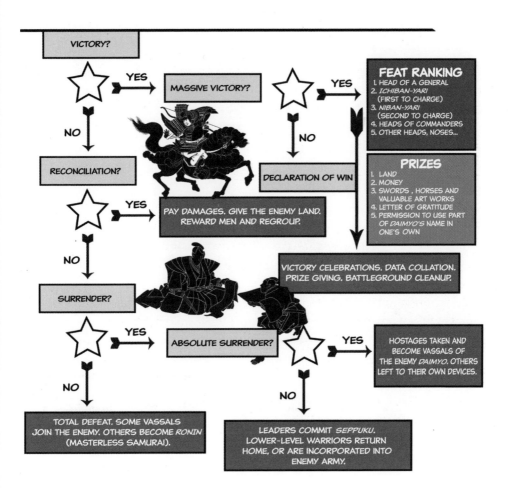

VICTORY?

→ NO → **RECONCILIATION?**

→ YES → **MASSIVE VICTORY?**

→ NO → **DECLARATION OF WIN**

→ YES → **FEAT RANKING**
1. HEAD OF A GENERAL
2. *ICHIBAN-YARI* (FIRST TO CHARGE)
3. *NIBAN-YARI* (SECOND TO CHARGE)
4. HEADS OF COMMANDERS
5. OTHER HEADS, NOSES...

PRIZES
1. LAND
2. MONEY
3. SWORDS , HORSES AND VALUABLE ART WORKS
4. LETTER OF GRATITUDE
5. PERMISSION TO USE PART OF *DAIMYO'S* NAME IN ONE'S OWN

→ YES → PAY DAMAGES. GIVE THE ENEMY LAND. REWARD MEN AND REGROUP.

→ NO → **SURRENDER?**

VICTORY CELEBRATIONS. DATA COLLATION. PRIZE GIVING. BATTLEGROUND CLEANUP.

→ YES → **ABSOLUTE SURRENDER?**

→ YES → HOSTAGES TAKEN AND BECOME VASSALS OF THE ENEMY *DAIMYO*. OTHERS LEFT TO THEIR OWN DEVICES.

→ NO → TOTAL DEFEAT. SOME VASSALS JOIN THE ENEMY. OTHERS BECOME *RONIN* (MASTERLESS SAMURAI).

→ NO → LEADERS COMMIT *SEPPUKU*. LOWER-LEVEL WARRIORS RETURN HOME, OR ARE INCORPORATED INTO ENEMY ARMY.

3. Weapons and Armor
The Bow

ARROW RELEASE

Most people consider the sword (*katana*) to be the Samurai's main weapon. Bows and arrows filled this role at first, and then pikes and firearms later. Mounted archery was the main form of Samurai combat until the emergence of massive infantry encounters during the Warring States period.

Warriors honed their skills in archery through practice methods such as *yabusame* (shooting boards at full gallop), *inuomono* (shooting dogs in a circle from horseback with blunted arrows), and *kasagake* (shooting targets). Skill in archery and the draw weight of the bow were defining elements in a warrior's reputation. So important was archery to Samurai identity that Samurai were originally called "adherents of the Way of the bow and arrow."

Swords

Straight, double-edged swords were first introduced into Japan from China in the ancient period (1st–8th centuries) and were used as implements in religious ceremonies. Around the 10th century, Japanese swordsmiths developed a distinctive style of forging and blade design, with curved, single-edged blades. These were slung as a sidearm to the left of the waist, with the cutting edge facing down. Referred to as *tachi*, swords were employed from horseback by high-ranking warriors when arrows were no longer an option.

From around the 14th century, Samurai adopted slightly shorter swords called *katana* inserted firmly through their belts, with the cutting blades facing up. The way they were worn allowed more stability for running and fighting on foot. Swords remained secondary weapons and were used for the rather grisly task of severing heads off corpses (*kubi-tori*).

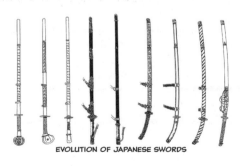

EVOLUTION OF JAPANESE SWORDS

Wearing a short and long sword as a set became the norm around the end of the Muromachi period. This was limited to the Samurai class after Toyotomi Hideyoshi's not entirely successful attempt to disarm the general population with his "Sword Hunt" of 1588. From around this time, swords became a symbol of Samurai status, but it was not until a decree issued by the Tokugawa shogunate in 1629 that wearing both swords became a mandatory and exclusive part of the Samurai's dress code.

Long Weapons

The *naginata* (glaive) was popular among early medieval Samurai. Essentially a sword attached to a long staff, *naginata* were useful for slashing or stabbing at horses or enemies from a distance but required skill to ensure that the blade hit the target on the correct angle to cut. Blades were prone to snapping, which is how the martial art

of *bojutsu*—the art of the long staff—came into being. The *naginata* was superseded in the 14th century with the introduction of pikes (*yari*), although it remained the weapon of choice for warrior-monks (*sohei*), and later became a martial skill studied by women of warrior families.

Weapons and battle scenes reproduced in Sasama, *Nihon Gassen Zuten*.

The *yari* was a simple weapon but it revolutionized medieval battlefields. Records indicate that from 1467 to 1600, the *yari* accounted for somewhere around 80 percent of inflicted casualties in close-quarters combat. The armies of the Warring States period employed huge regiments of semi-professional pike wielding peasant conscripts. The pike was cheap to produce and easier to brandish than traditional bladed weapons. Coordination rather than individual heroism was the key to success, and large mobile "walls" of pikemen proved to be formid-able barriers for charging horsemen. Pikes measured anywhere from 4.5 to 6.5 meters in length. They had straight metal tips with bladed edges and could be used to stab and slash from various ranges.

Firearms

Firearms are thought to have first entered Japan in 1543 when Portuguese adventurers visited the little southern island of Tanegashima. By the end of the 16th century, arquebuses were a vital weapon in any army. Oda Nobunaga is acknowledged as one of the first *daimyo* to adopt firearms and he used volleys of lead to devastating effect. Effectiveness aside, firearms were generally disliked by Samurai as "any monkey (peasant) can use them" to fell a superior warrior, and it was impossible to tell who scored the kill when it came to appraising feats of courage.

Unarmed Combat

Of course, the Samurai might find himself weaponless and needed to know how to subdue his enemy with his bare hands. Readers will know of Karate, a popular martial art which means "empty hand." The Samurai never studied Karate because it was a fighting system developed in Okinawa and never existed in mainland Japan until the 20th century. Instead, Samurai trained in the science of *jujutsu*, the "flexible art," a generic term for mostly unarmed wrestling or immobilization of an adversary. Other common terms were *yawara* and *kogu-soku*. Some systems incorporated small weapons such as daggers and practiced grappling in full armor. The *yawara* arts became less weapons-oriented with the onset of the peaceful Tokugawa period.

The fundamental principle for the technique is *ju-no-ri*, or the "law of yielding," that is, to combine one's physical power with the opponent's and use it against him rather than employ brute strength.

Yoroi

The earliest Japanese armor consisted of iron plates fastened together with leather cords. Elaborately decorated body armor with colorful panels (*o-yoroi*) appeared around the Heian period (794–1188) and was designed with mounted archery in mind. The protective flaps were pliable and light and enabled the warrior to release arrows from horseback from his left side. However, *o-yoroi* were not conducive to fighting on foot, and from the late 13th through to the mid-14th century a gradual transition was made to cheaper, lighter, wrap-around protection called *hara-maki*.

This coincided with the shift from mounted archers as the dominant combatants on battlefields. Simpler armor meant more stability and the option of using longer weapons like *yari* (pikes). Nevertheless, given the importance of being recognizable in the melee, Japanese armor and helmets (*kabuto*) were ostentatious and easily identifiable. They were meant to protect the warrior but also served as a kind of business card.

The armor of low-level foot soldiers was not nearly as ornate but was still functional, light, and emblazoned with clan insignia, and small banners at the back to help distinguish friend from foe.

The Emergence of Martial Art Schools (Ryuha)

The professional warrior was skilled in a variety of different weapons. Early martial arts in Japan were usually family affairs with tricks of the trade being passed on from father to son. It was not until the Muromachi period that we can see the rise of comprehensive martial schools known as *ryuha*. Curricula varied from school to school but typically included weapons training, divination, strategy, engineering, and even magic spells.

There were certain criteria that had to be met for the successful founding and continuation of a *ryuha*. A common element in most martial *ryuha* were stories of the founder being bequeathed secret knowledge by some deity. Preceding this

The time-consuming task of getting ready for battle.
Reproduced in Sasama, *Nihon Budo Jiten.*

religious revelation, the founder needed to have extensive battle experience and have earned a reputation for prowess that outshone his peers. Second, the combat procedures advanced by the founder needed to be effective and proven. Just as important, they also had to be teachable. This required a rational and sophisticated corpus of techniques that could be imitated by anybody who learned under the founder's tuition. Third, the founder needed to devise a practical system for passing on his knowledge so that apprentices could inherit the skills, thereby ensuring the school's continuation.

The traditional pedagogical methodology centered on individual instruction through the medium of predetermined technical sequences practiced in pairs (*kata*) pre-empting all manner of combat situations; oral teachings (*kuden*); and later on, codified scrolls (*densho*) that were purposefully vague to safeguard *ryuha* secrets from rival schools.

Given the secretive and pseudo-religious nature of these schools, disciples often accentuated the divine origins to enhance the perceived potency of its teachings, both technical and spiritual, and hence the reputation of its students. Typically, the highest level of knowledge (*hiden*) in a *ryuha* was esoteric, spiritual, and pragmatic. Being of divine origin, it held the key to the holy grail of combat through nurturing a synergy of body and mind and an outlook that transcended concerns of life and death.

The process of learning differed in each tradition, but universal principles such as the concept of *shu-ha-ri* applied. The instructions of the master were obediently followed in the *shu* (abide) stage. When the disciple had absorbed all he could from the master, he searched for his own interpretation by breaking away and testing his aptitude in duels with adherents from other schools (*ha*). After supplementing and enhancing his knowledge, and assuming he was still alive, he may acquire a profound understanding and receive his own divine visitation. Then he would independently create his own path (*ri*) and assemble his own followers.

Process for Creating a Martial Art School

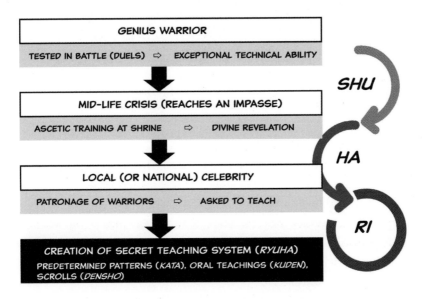

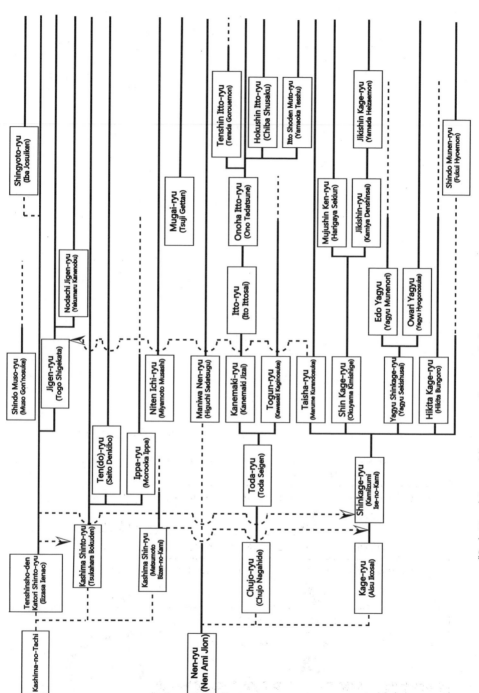

"Relationships and lineages of some of the prominent martial art schools."

Shingyoto-ryu
(Iba Josuiken)

Tenshin Itto-ryu
(Terada Gorouemon)

Hokushin Itto-ryu
(Chiba Shusaku)

Itto Shoden Muto-ryu
(Yamaoka Tesshu)

Jikishin Kage-ryu
(Yamada Heizaemon)

Shindo Munen-ryu
(Fukui Hyoemon)

Mugai-ryu
(Tsuji Gettan)

Onoha Itto-ryu
(Ono Tadatsune)

Mujushin Ken-ryu
(Harigaya Sekiun)

Jikishin-ryu
(Kamiya Denshinsai)

Nodachi Jigen-ryu
(Yakumaru Kanenobu)

Itto-ryu
(Ito Ittosai)

Edo Yagyu
(Yagyu Munenori)

Owari Yagyu
(Yagyu Hyogonosuke)

Shindo Muso-ryu
(Muso Gon'nosuke)

Jigen-ryu
(Togo Shigekata)

Niten Ichi-ryu
(Miyamoto Musashi)

Maniwa Nen-ryu
(Higuchi Sadatsugu)

Kanemaki-ryu
(Kanemaki Jizai)

Togun-ryu
(Kawasaki Kaginosuke)

Taisha-ryu
(Marume Kurandosuke)

Shin Kage-ryu
(Okuyama Kimishige)

Yagyu Shinkage-ryu
(Yagyu Sekishusai)

Hikita Kage-ryu
(Hikita Bungoro)

Ten(do)-ryu
(Saito Denkibo)

Ippa-ryu
(Morooka Ippa)

Tenshinsho-den
Katori Shinto-ryu
(Iizasa Ienao)

Kashima Shinto-ryu
(Tsukahara Bokuden)

Kashima Shin-ryu
(Matsumoto
Bizen-no-Kami)

Toda-ryu
(Toda Seigen)

Shinkage-ryu
(Kamiizumi
Ise-no-Kami)

Kashima-no-Tachi

Chujo-ryu
(Chujo Nagahide)

Kage-ryu
(Aisu Ikosai)

Nen-ryu
(Nen Ami Jion)

Honing combat ability in a *ryuha* was more than just a physical pursuit. It was akin to a lifelong form of artistic and religious training, hence the term *shugyo* (ascetic training), which is used in reference to training body and mind by both Samurai and Buddhist monks.

Although not limited to these, there are three main traditions acknowledged as having provided the core teachings for many hundreds of offshoot schools: Tenshinsho-den Katori Shinto-ryu, Nen-ryu, and Kage-ryu.

Yagyu Munenori and *Heiho Kadensho*

The martial arts and the warrior ethos are inextricably linked and both developed hand in hand. Yagyu Munenori (1571–1646) was an immensely influential martial artist active in the early Tokugawa period. Through his distinguished students in the Yagyu Shinkage-ryu, Munenori helped shape how the Samurai redefined their role in peacetime.

Munenori was the son of the renowned Warring States period swordsman Yagyu Muneyoshi, founder of the Yagyu Shinkage-ryu school (stemming from the Kage-ryu tradition) and student of the legendary Kamiizumi Ise-no-Kami. Munenori proved his worth in battle at the summer siege of Osaka Castle in 1615. Well regarded by Tokugawa Ieyasu, Munenori's students included the second and third Tokugawa shoguns, Hidetada and Iemitsu. With such illustrious patronage, combined with his pedigree in swordsmanship, high-ranked Samurai, including *daimyo* and their retainers, sought out his instruction.

In 1632, Muneyori completed the *Heiho Kadensho*, a comprehensive treatise on swordsmanship, which he wrote for the shogun Iemitsu. The content is a complex blending of Muneyoshi's and Kamiizumi Ise-no-Kami's teachings on swordsmanship derived from Noh and Zen principles. His dissertation was copied and distributed among his powerful disciples as a textbook for their study of Yagyu Shinkage-ryu swordsmanship and as a guide to how it could be applied to governance.

Heiho Kadensho is divided into the three sections: *Shinrikyo* ("shoe-offering bridge"), *Setsunin-to* ("death-dealing blade"), and *Katsunin-ken* ("life-giving sword"). *Shinrikyo* is a catalogue of the school's techniques and consists of the three categories of *jo*, *ha*, and *kyu*, each containing nine techniques. The remaining sections are philosophical expositions on the psychological aspects of swordsmanship and how the underpinning philosophy and moral considerations of combat are relevant to political rule.

The War and Peace Paradox

殺人刀 (*SETSUNIN-TO*)
DEATH-DEALING BLADE

刀 = *TO* = SINGLE-EDGED BLADE DIRECTED AT THE ENEMY

剣 = *KEN* = DOUBLE-EDGED BLADE DIRECTED AT THE SELF AS WELL

活人剣 (*KATSUJIN-KEN*)
LIFE-GIVING SWORD

SAMURAI MUST KNOW THE TECHNIQUES OF KILLING

AT TIMES BECAUSE OF ONE MAN'S EVIL TEN THOUSAND PEOPLE SUFFER. SO YOU KILL THAT ONE MAN TO LET TENS OF THOUSANDS LIVE

HERE, TRULY, THE BLADE THAT DEALS DEATH BECOMES THE SWORD THAT SAVES LIVES

KNOWING HOW TO KILL, SAMURAI MUST ONLY USE FORCE AS A LAST RESORT

In *Setsunin-to*, Munenori states that weapons are wicked as they cause death and destruction and contravene the "Way of Heaven" (*tendo*). Nevertheless, he acknowledges that there are times when violent force is unavoidable for maintaining peace: "Killing one man's evil so that ten thousand may live." In order to "kill one man's evil," the warrior needs to excel in the art of war. He further explains that regardless of the scale of the conflict, be it one-on-one combat or pitched battle, victory or defeat is determined by how well the warrior has mastered the principles of strategy. Strategy employed in the smallest encounter between two warriors is in essence the same as that utilized by the shogun directing his realm.

It is *heiho* (combat strategy) to be aware of disorder when ruling the country in a time of peace. Likewise, it is *heiho* to scrutinize the internal workings of the realm to understand what turmoil is, and to rule the people effectively before chaos erupts.

"It is a limited mind," argued Munenori, "that considers swordsmanship and military studies just as a means for killing. They are not for cutting people down in as much as they are tools to rid the world of evil. This is how ten thousand men can be given life by killing a single man." This is also how the death-dealing blade becomes the life-giving sword. *Heiho Kadensho* was the first significant treatise in Japan to link the training of body and mind in a martial art into a systematic holistic corpus for life and governance.

Yagyu Shinkage-ryu Curriculum

天道＝活人剣

TENDO = HEAVEN'S WAY = *KATSUJIN-KEN*. THIS IS THE HIGHEST LEVEL OF TECHNICAL, POLITICAL AND SPIRITUAL PERFECTION WHERE THE PARADOX OF "WAR EQUALS PEACE" IS ACHIEVED, AND THE "DEATH-DEALING BLADE" BECOMES THE "LIFE-GIVING SWORD".

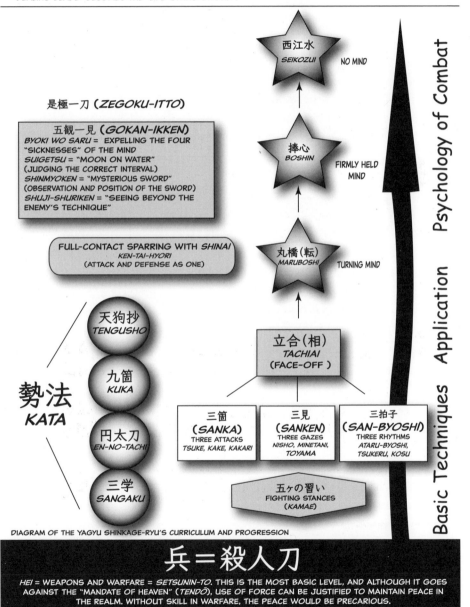

西江水
SEIKOZUI

NO MIND

是極一刀 (*ZEGOKU-ITTO*)

五観一見 (*GOKAN-IKKEN*)
BYOKI WO SARU = EXPELLING THE FOUR "SICKNESSES" OF THE MIND
SUIGETSU = "MOON ON WATER" (JUDGING THE CORRECT INTERVAL)
SHINMYOKEN = "MYSTERIOUS SWORD" (OBSERVATION AND POSITION OF THE SWORD)
SHUJI-SHURIKEN = "SEEING BEYOND THE ENEMY'S TECHNIQUE"

捧心
BOSHIN

FIRMLY HELD MIND

FULL-CONTACT SPARRING WITH *SHINAI*
KEN-TAI-HYORI
(ATTACK AND DEFENSE AS ONE)

丸橋 (転)
MARUBOSHI

TURNING MIND

天狗抄
TENGUSHO

九箇
KUKA

勢法
KATA

円太刀
EN-NO-TACHI

三学
SANGAKU

立合 (相)
TACHIAI
(FACE-OFF)

三箇
(*SANKA*)
THREE ATTACKS
TSUKE, KAKE, KAKARI

三見
(*SANKEN*)
THREE GAZES
NISHO, MINETANI, TOYAMA

三拍子
(*SAN-BYOSHI*)
THREE RHYTHMS
ATARU-BYOSHI, TSUKERU, KOSU

五ヶの習い
FIGHTING STANCES
(*KAMAE*)

DIAGRAM OF THE YAGYU SHINKAGE-RYU'S CURRICULUM AND PROGRESSION

Psychology of Combat

Application

Basic Techniques

兵＝殺人刀

HEI = WEAPONS AND WARFARE = *SETSUNIN-TO*. THIS IS THE MOST BASIC LEVEL, AND ALTHOUGH IT GOES AGAINST THE "MANDATE OF HEAVEN" (*TENDŌ*), USE OF FORCE CAN BE JUSTIFIED TO MAINTAIN PEACE IN THE REALM. WITHOUT SKILL IN WARFARE, THE PEACE WOULD BE PRECARIOUS.

Miyamoto Musashi and *Gorin-no-sho*

Arguably the most celebrated warrior in Japanese history, Miyamoto Musashi (1582–1645) was born in Harima as the second son of Tahara Iesada. He had his first taste of combat at the age of thirteen when he challenged and killed Arima Kihei of the Shinto-ryu. He spent the next fifteen years as an itinerant swordsman dueling his way to notoriety. Musashi established the Enmei-ryu school in 1605. He renamed his style of swordsmanship *Nito Ichi-ryu* ("The School of Two Swords as One"), and finally *Niten Ichi-ryu* ("Two Heavens One School") because "all warriors, from general to rank-and-file, are duty bound to wear two swords in their belts," so warriors must know the merits of carrying two swords.

The best-known of his sixty odd duels was in 1610 against Ganryu Kojiro on an island called Funajima (later called Ganryujima). After defeating Kojiro, he realized that his success and survival thus far were due more to luck than to any genuine knowledge. He decided to spend the rest of his life in pursuit of a greater truth, and after many years of austere training came to understand that the principles for success in combat are the same as for all aspects of life.

Musashi is credited with several books related to the martial arts, including *Heidokyo* (1605), *Heiho Kakitsuke* (1638), *Heiho Sanjugo-kajo* (1641), *Dokkodo* (1645), and the most famous of all, *Gorin-no-Sho* (1645) which he wrote for his students in Kumamoto's Reigando cave, handing it over one week before he died.

Chapters in Gorin-no-Sho

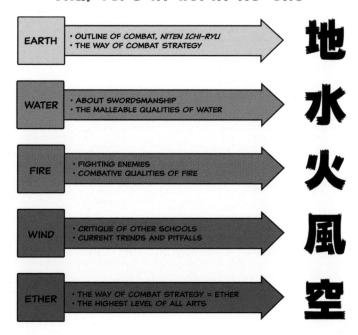

EARTH	• OUTLINE OF COMBAT, *NITEN ICHI-RYU* • THE WAY OF COMBAT STRATEGY
WATER	• ABOUT SWORDSMANSHIP • THE MALLEABLE QUALITIES OF WATER
FIRE	• FIGHTING ENEMIES • COMBATIVE QUALITIES OF FIRE
WIND	• CRITIQUE OF OTHER SCHOOLS • CURRENT TRENDS AND PITFALLS
ETHER	• THE WAY OF COMBAT STRATEGY = ETHER • THE HIGHEST LEVEL OF ALL ARTS

地

水

火

風

空

Gorin-no-Sho (Book of Five Rings) consists of five chapters or "scrolls": *Chi* (earth), *Sui* (water), *Ka* (fire), *Fu* (wind), and *Ku* (Ether). In the Earth scroll, Musashi documents the first half of his life. He also includes an introduction to military tactics and the philosophy behind the school he created. In the Water scroll, Musashi explains various aspects of individual combat, such as mental and physical posture, gaze, manipulating the sword, footwork, and fighting stances. In Fire, he expounds how to choose the best site for dueling, how to control the enemy by taking the initiative, and how to implement strategies.

In the fourth scroll, Wind, he critiques other schools of swordsmanship and outlines their weaknesses. Ether is a short but decidedly complicated section where Musashi delves into how he developed the Niten Ichi-ryu. He discloses the supreme level of combat and all arts by referring to the allegorical "void." "Having comprehended the truth of the Way, you can then let it go. You will find liberation in the Way of combat strategy and naturally attain a marvelous capacity to know the most rational rhythm for every moment. Your strike will manifest on its own and hit the target on its own. All this represents the Way of the Ether."

Musashi taught that in the "Way of combat strategy," overlooking the most fundamental matters will hold the warrior back. By dedicating all of his energies to learning swordsmanship via the "Direct Way," the warrior will learn to "defeat men through superior technique, and even beat them just by looking with your eyes. Your body will learn to move freely through the rigors of arduous training and you will also overcome your opponent physically. Furthermore, with your spirit attuned to the Way you will triumph over the enemy with your mind. Having come so far, how can you be beaten by anyone?"

He observed that in the practice of all arts, struggling in the pursuit of the true Way, allowing one's mind to wander even a little, leads to a colossal deviation. "Inquiring into the minds of Samurai today, it would seem that many believe the warrior's Way demands nothing more than an unwavering preparedness for death."

Musashi contends that all people are prepared to sacrifice their life when the time comes. The only difference in the warrior's Way compared to others is that the "warrior must win." There are no second chances.

When Musashi wrote *Gorin-no-Sho*, the country had not seen war for over a decade, and there was thus a generation of Samurai who had never experienced battle first hand. Perhaps this was an admonition to his students that true mortal combat was not something to be understood conceptually, and therefore unfounded arrogance in such matters would lead them down the wrong path. The important thing was to engage with single-minded resolve. The ability to do this would open the mind to a profound understanding of all things.

Musashi's "Way" of Combat

"IRRESPECTIVE OF THE WAY, KNOWING HOW NOT TO LOSE TO OTHERS AND ESTABLISHING YOURSELF IN NAME AND STATURE IS PARAMOUNT. THIS IS PRECISELY WHAT THE WAY OF COMBAT STRATEGY IS." (EARTH)

I.E. TO EXCEL AT SOMETHING LIKE POETRY, COMBAT, FARMING... THERE ARE MANY WAYS...

- CHOOSE YOUR WAY
- MASTER THAT WAY
- GOING YOUR WAY

"LOVE YOUR WAY" = ALL OR NOTHING FORGE YOUR PATH AS IF LIFE DEPENDED ON IT (BECAUSE IT DID!)

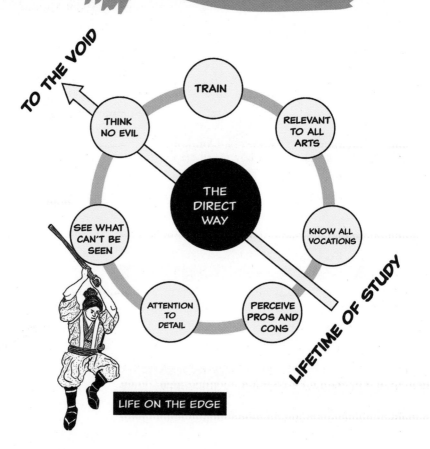

TO THE VOID

TRAIN

THINK NO EVIL

RELEVANT TO ALL ARTS

THE DIRECT WAY

SEE WHAT CAN'T BE SEEN

KNOW ALL VOCATIONS

ATTENTION TO DETAIL

PERCEIVE PROS AND CONS

LIFETIME OF STUDY

LIFE ON THE EDGE

The Way
The Perils of Being Negligent

COLORFUL DISPLAYS OF TECHNIQUE ARE FLAUNTED IN THESE [FALSE] MARTIAL ART "WAYS" TO FORCE THE FLOWER INTO BLOOM. PROFITEERS BLATHERING OVER THIS *DOJO* OR THAT *DOJO*, TEACHING ONE WAY OR LEARNING ANOTHER IN THE HOPE OF CONQUERING IN THE FRAY, FITS THE [POPULAR] ADAGE "UNRIPE MARTIAL ARTS ARE THE ROOT OF SERIOUS HARM." (EARTH)

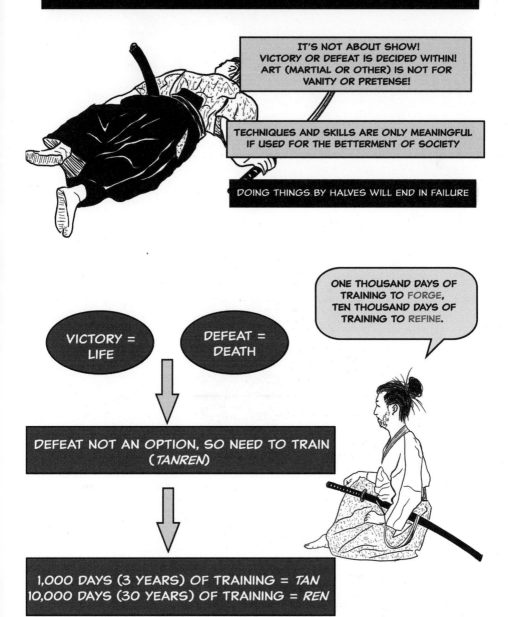

IT'S NOT ABOUT SHOW!
VICTORY OR DEFEAT IS DECIDED WITHIN!
ART (MARTIAL OR OTHER) IS NOT FOR VANITY OR PRETENSE!

TECHNIQUES AND SKILLS ARE ONLY MEANINGFUL IF USED FOR THE BETTERMENT OF SOCIETY

DOING THINGS BY HALVES WILL END IN FAILURE

ONE THOUSAND DAYS OF TRAINING TO FORGE, TEN THOUSAND DAYS OF TRAINING TO REFINE.

VICTORY = LIFE

DEFEAT = DEATH

DEFEAT NOT AN *OPTION*, SO NEED TO TRAIN (*TANREN*)

1,000 DAYS (3 YEARS) OF TRAINING = *TAN*
10,000 DAYS (30 YEARS) OF TRAINING = *REN*

Musashi was relentless in his own study and urged his students to be patient as they learned the virtue of all phenomena "utilizing every opportunity to accumulate actual experience" as they traverse "the thousand-mile road one step at a time." He advised there was no need for haste in training, but instead "seek victory today over the self of yesterday," mindful of keeping strictly to the path.

"Even if you defeat the most daunting of adversaries, if your victories are not in accord with the principles contained within these scrolls, then they cannot be considered true to the Way." It was through embracing the principles of the Way that the swordsman could prevail over dozens of men. Mastering the art of combat for individual duels was the same as that of large-scale strategy for battle. But this took time. "One-thousand days of training to forge, ten-thousand days of training to refine."

The correct attitude in the Way of combat must be no different from one's normal state of mind. "In the course of your daily life, and when engaged in strategy, there should be no change whatsoever in your outlook. Your mind should be expansive and direct, devoid of tension, but not at all casual," that is, keep the mind centered, "swaying serenely and freely so that it does not come to a standstill in moments of change."

Attitude of Combat

1. THINK NEVER TO VEER FROM THE WAY
2. TRAIN UNREMITTINGLY IN THE WAY
3. ACQUAINT YOURSELF WITH ALL ARTS
4. KNOW THE WAYS OF ALL VOCATIONS
5. DISCERN THE TRUTH IN ALL THINGS
6. SEE THE INTRINSIC WORTH IN ALL THINGS
7. PERCEIVE AND KNOW WHAT CANNOT BE SEEN WITH THE EYES
8. PAY ATTENTION EVEN TO TRIFLES
9. DO NOT ENGAGE IN SUPERFLUOUS ACTIVITIES

| POWERS OF JUDGMENT OBSERVATION ABSORBING | → | ATTENTION TO DETAIL EFFICIENCY PREPARATION |

兵法の道

The Way of Combat
is the Way of Everything

"Looking In" and "Looking At"

ONE'S GAZE SHOULD BE EXPANSIVE AND FAR-REACHING. THIS IS THE DUAL GAZE OF "LOOKING IN" (*KAN*) AND "LOOKING AT" (*KEN*). THE GAZE FOR "LOOKING IN" IS INTENSE WHEREAS THAT FOR "LOOKING AT" IS GENTLE. IT IS OF UTMOST IMPORTANCE FOR A WARRIOR TO SEE DISTANT THINGS AS IF THEY WERE CLOSE AND CLOSE THINGS AS IF THEY WERE DISTANT. (WATER)

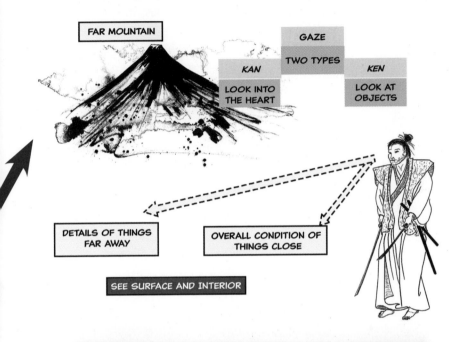

FAR MOUNTAIN

GAZE
TWO TYPES

KAN
LOOK INTO THE HEART

KEN
LOOK AT OBJECTS

DETAILS OF THINGS FAR AWAY

OVERALL CONDITION OF THINGS CLOSE

SEE SURFACE AND INTERIOR

Cadence (*Hyoshi*)
Rhythm, timing, tempo, tone, momentum, vitality, breathing, distance...

TYPICAL CADENCE = DANCE, MUSIC, CLAPPING BEAT, MUSICAL RHYTHM

INVISIBLE CADENCE = CADENCE OF SUCCESS, FAILURE, PROSPERITY, DECAY, WAVES OF WEAKNESS AND STRENGTH

REVERSE CADENCE, OPPOSING CADENCE, DETACHED CADENCE...

COMBAT CADENCE = OPPONENT'S FOOTWORK, MOVEMENT OF THE SWORD, BREATHING PATTERNS, SPIRIT (BIG, SMALL, SLOW, FAST)

Musashi is very matter of fact in his technical explanations. He also emphasizes psychological details and the importance of powers of concentration and the ability to observe all things unimpeded. "The swordsman must learn to polish the two layers of his mind." Musashi explains these layers as the "heart of perception" and the "heart of intent," the two gazes of *kan* ("looking in") and *ken* ("looking at"). One's gaze should be expansive and far-reaching. This is the dual gaze of "looking in" and "looking at." It is as if one is looking at something close to you as a mountain far away, taking in its entire shape while perceiving something that is far away as if it were very close.

The gaze for "looking in" is intense whereas that for "looking at" is gentle. "It is of utmost importance for a warrior to see distant things as if they were close and close things as if they were distant." It is vital to be able to see both without needing to move the eyes.

Central to Musashi's swordsmanship was using this perception to identify the rhythm inherent in all things. "First, the warrior must know the cadence of harmony and then learn those of discord. He must know the striking, interval and counter cadences that manifest among big and small, fast and slow rhythms."

He declares how it is critical for success to know how to adopt "counter rhythms" to what the enemy is doing. "You must discern cadences of various enemies and employ a rhythm that is unexpected to them. Use your wisdom to detect and strike concealed cadences to seize victory."

Musashi states he was about fifty when he realized the true meaning of the Way. "Having attained the essence of the Way of combat strategy, I practice the disciplines of many arts without the need of a teacher in any of them." Indeed, Musashi was a talented artist, and some of his paintings remain today in Japan as National Treasures. He attributes this to tapping the "Ether," a place where there is nothing. "I consider this emptiness as something which cannot be known. Of course, Ether is also nothing. Knowing what does exist, one can then know what does not." Ether is not something that cannot be distinguished, nor is it a description of various doubts that are harbored in the mind. By scrupulously learning by heart the Way of combat strategy and thoroughly studying other martial arts without forgoing any aspect related to the practice of the warrior's Way, the Samurai must seek to "put the Way into practice each hour of every day without tiring or losing focus." Only then can the true Ether become apparent, "where all the clouds of confusion have completely lifted, leaving not a hint of haziness."

As his final teaching, he implores his students to "Make the sincere heart your Way as you practice strategy in its broadest sense, correctly and lucidly. Ponder the Ether as you study the Way. As you practice the Way, the Ether will open before you."

The Ultimate Realm in All Arts

- THOROUGHLY KNOW THE WAY OF COMBAT STRATEGY
- KNOW VARIOUS ARTS
- A MIND THAT NEVER WAIVERS
- POLISH THE TWO LAYERS OF THE MIND, "HEART OF PERCEPTION" AND "HEART OF INTENT"
- "LOOK IN" (WITH THE HEART) AND "LOOK AT" (WITH THE EYES)

THERE IS GOOD, NOT EVIL IN THE ETHER
THERE IS WISDOM, THERE IS REASON
THERE IS THE WAY, THE MIND, EMPTY

ETHER

A PLACE WHERE THERE IS NOTHING

CLOUDS OF CONFUSION

WHEN THE SPIRIT IS UNCURLED AND COMPARED WITH OVERARCHING UNIVERSAL PRINCIPLES, IT BECOMES EVIDENT THAT A PREJUDICED MIND AND A DISTORTED VIEW OF THINGS HAVE LED TO A DEPARTURE FROM THE PROPER PATH.

CRAFT

POETRY

COMBAT

PAINTING

CARVING

There is Good, not Evil in the Ether
There is Wisdom
There is Reason
There is the Way
The Mind, Empty

The Evolution of Martial Arts

With the onset of the Tokugawa shogunate, opportunities for warriors to display their fighting skill dried up. However, they were still expected to study the military arts even if the practical necessity no longer seemed apparent. Military drill was indispensable for maintaining a sense of self-identity as well as for providing the symbolic basis for class identity. After all, their culture of honor, matured over many centuries, was based on martial ability.

Bakufu sanctions to control violence acted as a catalyst for the progression of martial arts from techniques for killing to "Ways" of self-perfection, and ultimately to what can be termed "spiritual sports." Participation provided recourse to controlled expression of pent-up tensions, and the excitement of mock battle helped warriors preserve their elitist collective identity *vis-à-vis* other classes.

A number of distinct trends are evident in martial arts during the Tokugawa period, particularly swordsmanship. These included Intellectualization; Spiritualization and pacification; Commercialization; and, finally, Sportification.

The number of martial art schools proliferated exponentially from around the late 1600s to meet market demand for proof of military preparedness. They tended to specialize in specific weapons rather than a variety, unlike in previous more turbulent eras. Sword schools were by far the most prolific.

The techniques practiced in pairs (*kata*) became increasingly ostentatious and removed from the realities of actual combat. Elaborate and obscure philosophies were concocted by the headmasters of new schools to accompany the techniques, giving military drill an increasingly spiritual quality as the focus moved away from combat efficiency to "Ways" of augmenting spiritual development and self-discipline.

The invention of protective training equipment around the start of the 18th century gave rise to "full-contact" training methods instead of just choreographed *kata*. Martial artists could now compete to score "death blows" on each other without the bloody consequences. This was the beginning of "martial sports."

Bugei Juhappan

Bugei juhappan literally means the "eighteen martial arts" that were studied by Samurai during the Tokugawa period. The concept originated in China but came to represent all the martial arts in Japan, not just eighteen. A common term in the Tokugawa period, the so-called "Eighteen" martial arts, depended on the feudal domain (*ryuha*) that practiced its own style. The following are usually cited:

1. *Kyujutsu* (archery)
2. *Bajutsu* (horsemanship)
3. *Suijutsu* (swimming)
4. *Naginata-jutsu* (glaivemanship)
5. *Sojutsu* (pikemanship)
6. *Kenjutsu* (swordsmanship)
7. *Kogusoku* (grappling with armor on)
8. *Bojutsu* (using a long staff)
9. *Jojutsu* (using a short staff)
10. *Kusarigama-jutsu* (using a sickle and chain)
11. *Fundo-kusari* (using a weighted chain)
12. *Shuriken-jutsu* (using hand-held projectile weapons)
13. *Fukumibari-jutsu* (spitting needles)
14. *Jutte-jutsu* (using a truncheon)
15. *Iaijutsu* or *battojutsu* (sword drawing)
16. *Jujutsu* (grappling)
17. *Mojiri-jutsu* (using a barbed staff or bear-hand)
18. *Sasumata-jutsu* (using a fork spear)
19. *Shinobi* (intelligence gathering and espionage)
20. *Hojutsu* (gunmanship)

Martial Arts as Vehicles for Self-perfection

In times of social tumult, spiritual fortitude and transcendence were ways of dealing with the reality of death, but in times of peace martial training transformed into an intrinsic part of nurturing individual morality and self-control rather than the ability or will to actually kill.

Influential books in the category of "martial spiritualism" include Niwa Jurozaemon Tadaaki's *Neko-no-Myojutsu* (1729). Tadaaki was a gifted student in Zen, Confucian, and Chinese classics as well as the martial arts. *Neko-no-Myojutsu* (The Cat's Eerie Skills) is an entertaining story of a large rat that torments the local cats with his defiant behavior. Each cat tries to outdo the other and capture the bold rat, but none is successful. An aged cat then decides to take up the challenge and captures the rat with seemingly no effort.

The other cats are amazed and ask how he did it. The narrative then turns to the wise old cat educating his much younger protégés. He talks of the natural way of the universe (*dori*) and the use of *ki* (vital force or life energy), and how the warrior who can maintain control over his mind and access the very essence of his existence will be able to triumph in all things.

All the cats gather around and a discussion commences. First, the young black cat relays how he had practiced his skills since he was a young cat by running through the rafters, and that he had never failed to catch a rat until this day. The old cat replies that his problem was being too focused on developing technical skill, and that he was preoccupied with the "art." Next, the big cat with tiger's whiskers asserts his belief that *ki* is of the essence in martial arts. He tells of how he had spent years developing his *ki*, and how he can use it to overpower his opponents but was unable to achieve this against the rat today. The old cat points out that relying on the powers of *ki* alone will not work against an opponent who refuses to play the game.

The Cat's Eerie Skill

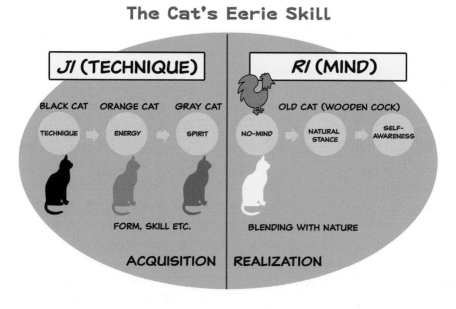

Next, the gray, slightly older cat steps forward and explains that he trained for a long time in the Way and learned how to win by non-confrontation. However, the rat today was not tempted by his peaceful advances. The old cat suggests that he was not in harmony with nature. He was conspiring with a conscious mind and therefore was ineffectual. The old cat continues by preaching how all forms have their opposites. We exist, therefore so does the enemy. "If we have no form in our minds, nothing can oppose it and there will be no conflict. Namely, there is no enemy." In the final analysis, the problem lies in the mind, but if the mind is in a state of *mushin* (no-mind), there can be no foe.

As an example, he refers to stages of training using a similar story to that of the wooden cock recorded in Lao Tzu's writings. Starting with the development of technical skill, the next stage requires the strengthening of psychic or spiritual power, then the realization of the importance of yielding, and finally the enlightened stage of the wooden cock. At the final stage, there is no foe, and the reason is explained through a process culminating with supreme knowledge and enlightened clarity that comes from age and experience. This is similar to Musashi's concept of the Ether.

From around this time, the mid-Tokugawa era, the interpretation of *bu* (武) (martial) also evolved to paradoxically mean "anti-war." Originally, the character is said to consist of the radicals for "foot" (足) or possibly "to walk" (歩) with "lance" (矛) in hand. In other words, the ideogram was alluding to foot soldiers marching off to battle. From around the middle of the Tokugawa period, it began to be construed pacifistically as "to stop" (止) fighting with the "lance" (矛).

Seppuku (Harakiri)

It is believed that Minamoto-no-Yorimasa performed the first act of *seppuku*, or ritual suicide by self-disembowelment, during the Battle of Uji in 1180. He probably committed suicide in this way to demonstrate his prowess and to avert torture at the hands of his enemies. Over time, *seppuku* became an established part of Samurai culture. For example, in the Warring States period, conquered *daimyo* were sometimes required to commit *seppuku* to honorably confirm the clan's submission. Later, warriors who had transgressed the boundaries of acceptable behavior were given the privilege of dying by their own hand rather than the humiliation of execution, in order to restore their honor.

Seppuku became a legal and ceremonial institution over time, a means by which warriors could expiate their crimes, apologize for errors, escape from disgrace, redeem their friends, or prove their veracity. Nobody could perform the excruciating act without the utmost composure, and it was appraised by witnesses who rated the degree of self-control displayed by the condemned warrior.

Reserved for Samurai, *seppuku* became a highly ritualized procedure around the 17th century. A *kaishakunin* (assistant) was utilized to deal the mercy stroke after the Samurai had plunged the blade into his abdomen. Prior to this, the Samurai would finish himself off by stabbing himself in the throat or falling on his sword.

Seppuku

Junshi: Following one's lord in death
Kanshi: Suicide as remonstration
Sokotsu-shi: Making amends

EXPIATE CRIMES

REDEEM FRIENDS OR LORD

SEPPUKU

APOLOGIZE FOR ERRORS

I WILL OPEN THE SEAT OF MY SOUL AND SHOW YOU HOW IT FARES WITHIN. SEE FOR YOURSELF WHETHER IT IS POLLUTED OR CLEAN.

PROVE SINCERITY

ESCAPE DISGRACE

Legal and ceremonial

A close friend or relative was often called upon to fill the role of *kaishakunin*, whose job was not that of an executioner. Once the Samurai, traditionally dressed in white robes as a sign of purity, had made a horizontal cut across his gut, he would extend his neck to signal his readiness for decapitation. A skilled *kaishaki-nin* would cut through the neck leaving a tab of skin on the throat so that the head did not fly into the official witnesses. As a side note, *seppuku* was deferred if the *Samurai* had an upset stomach.

Vengeance

Katakiuchi, or revenge for the killing of a relation or superior, was justified and even lauded throughout much of Japan's history. The model for this practice harks back to the tale of the two Soga brothers who exacted revenge for the murder of their father in 1193. Vendettas became increasingly common during the medieval period and continued into the Tokugawa period even though violence was strictly sanctioned. As long as he who sought revenge registered his intent with the authorities beforehand, successful completion of this blood mission would make the exacter a hero of sorts.

Seeking Vengeance

LODGES A FORMAL COMPLAINT AND INTENT TO EXACT REVENGE

SHOGUN DEPUTY'S OFFICE IN KYOTO OR CENTRAL AUTHORITY IN EDO

INTENT REGISTERED AND PERMISSION GRANTED

EMBARKS ON QUEST TO FIND AVOWED ENEMY

LEDGER OF PUBLIC AFFAIRS

仇

KATAKI

DISCOVERS HIS WHEREABOUTS

KILLS HIM IN A DUEL

MISSION ACCOMPLISHED

BECOMES A CELEBRITY FOR HIS CONVICTION AND VALOR JOB OFFERS?

As Nitobe Inazo wrote regarding matters of redress, "In revenge there is something which satisfies one's sense of justice." The avenger reasons, "My good father did not deserve death.... Heaven itself hates wrongdoing. It is the will of my father; it is the will of Heaven that the evil-doer ceases from his work. He must perish by my hand; because he shed my father's blood, I, who am his flesh and blood, must shed the murderer's. The same Heaven shall not shelter him and me."

There were various rules in place to prevent unwanted escalation of violence. For example, a vendetta was not allowed to continue after the first revenge killing was accomplished. Moreover, it could only be directed at the perpetrator of the original murder, not other members of his household. The practice was abolished with the introduction of a modern legal code in 1873.

The best-known vendetta of the Tokugawa period was that of the "Forty-Seven Ronin." It is celebrated as a prime example of the warrior virtue of loyalty. The incident took place after two years of planning in the early hours of January 31, 1703. Former retainers of lord Asano Naganori (1665–1701) of Ako stormed the residence of Kira Yoshinaka and assassinated him to avenge the wrong they believed had been done to their lord resulting in his condemnation by the shogun and death by *seppuku*. This vendetta was carried out in secret and was an audacious contravention of the law. Favorable public opinion of their actions persuaded the shogun to allow the *ronin* to commit *seppuku* as the honorable conclusion to the incident rather than execution as common criminals.

Painting of Oishi Yoshio, one of the leaders of the Forty-Seven Ronin, committing seppuku. (Wikimedia Commons)

Chapter 3
The Medieval Warrior Ethos
中世武士の思想

As noted in Chapter 1, Ashikaga Takauji established Japan's second shogunate in the Muromachi district of Kyoto. This sparked an influx of Samurai from the provinces to the ancient capital. Their presence was not welcomed by the nobles, who ostracized the Samurai as uncouth ruffians. Perhaps motivated by a kind of cultural inferiority complex, the upper-echelon Samurai, in particular, turned their attention to cultivating a sense of decorum and artistic appreciation and behaving in a more sophisticated way than life in the provinces required.

This trend is evident in two developments during the Muromachi period: the proliferation of "house codes" (*kakun*) and the dissemination of manuals outlining special Samurai ceremonies and rules of conduct (*buke kojitsu*), which trace their origins to the customs of the ancient imperial court. Samurai had already created their own conventions and ceremonial forms during the Kamakura period but it took on more urgency after their relocation to Kyoto. The content of the manuals included various rules relating to appropriate dress, etiquette for everyday interaction, and general expectations for the ideal warrior.

As the term indicates, "house codes" contained advice for clan members. A common characteristic was concern for balancing martial aptitude with knowledge in the refined arts, that is, an equilibrium between *bu* (martial) and *bun* (letters or the arts), or the "brush and sword in accord." Samurai aspired to be worthy of their supreme position through intellect and civility, although violence was always an effective backup plan.

These codes of behavior were primarily written by the clan patriarch to ensure his descendants avoided committing any embarrassment in the warrior community of honor. In his *kakun* of 1412, Imagawa Ryoshun, for example, declares "It is natural that Samurai learn the ways of war and apply themselves to the acquisition of the basic fighting skills needed for their occupation. However, it is clearly stated in ancient military texts such as the *Shishi Gokyo* (The Four Books and Five Classics) that without applying oneself to study [of the civil arts], it is impossible to be a worthy ruler...."

Another well-known *kakun*, Shiba Yoshimasa's *Chikubasho* (1383), also urges the ruling class to pay attention to matters of propriety, self-cultivation, attention to detail, and to take care in speech "so as not to be thought an ass by others...." Yoshimasa, like many of his contemporaries, espouses the importance of being familiar with such diversions as linked verse and playing musical instruments, in addition to the martial arts.

A much later house code is the "99 Precepts" of the Takeda clan, drawn up in 1558 by Takeda Nobushige. The content is remarkably practical, with down to earth advice such as "Do not praise the enemy for their greatness in front of one's own troops." "Do not let one's men defame the enemy [and thereby enrage them]." "Do not show a weak attitude even in front of relatives or attendants." "When deploying troops, it is necessary to discern what enemy to make peace with, what enemy to destroy, and what enemy to conquer." And at number 98, "Always be alert."

This house code is contained in an important chronicle that offers fascinating insights into the precarious reality of Samurai during the Warring States period. The encyclopedic *Koyo-gunkan* about the Takeda clan is peppered with practical teachings to ensure survival in a world where today's friend is tomorrow's enemy. The overarching theme of *Koyo-gunkan* is "avoidance of excess." Warriors must never go to extremes, it warned, as balance in everything was paramount. The most obvious task in the Warring States period was to hone military skills, but the *Koyo-gunkan* also urges that this must be accompanied by compassion. For warriors who navigated the precipice between life and death, such awareness provided the key to survival.

This chapter will look at some notable compositions on warrior ideals of the tempestuous medieval period. It is these works that Samurai of the Tokugawa period referred to nostalgically while adjusting to their new role in a more civilized time.

Hojo Shigetoki (1198–1261)
北条重時

1. The Brush and the Sword

Apart from two interesting letters, "Letter to Nagatoki" (1247) and the "Gokur-akuji Letter" (1256), not much information is available about Hojo Shigetoki in historical sources. He was appointed to the position of Kyoto deputy overseer (*tandai*) between 1230 and 1247 and served on the council of state. Consisting of forty-three articles, "Letter to Nagatoki" was written to his son Nagatoki, giving advice when he took over his father's role of Kyoto *tandai* in 1247. It deals more with manners and procedures rather than any proposed moral outlook. Advice such as "not talking about important matters with unintelligent servants" and "never letting them see you in your underwear" are somewhat amusing exhorta-tions!

The "Gokurakuji Letter" is more substantial. Containing ninety-eight articles, it was composed at the Gokurakuji Temple located just outside Kamakura where Shigetoki retired in his twilight years. It also offers directives on correct behavior but also expounds on a distinct way of life. Both of these letters are categorized as house codes (*kakun*). It could be said that Shigetoki was one of the first warriors to embrace the ideal of "brush and sword in accord" as a defining quality for Samurai.

A striking feature of the "Gokurakuji Letter" is the emphasis Shigetoki places on Buddhist thought. He describes how the world is impermanent and everything in life is transient and guided by karma. Thus, he advises that the warrior be aware of his actions in the present as they will dictate his future incarnation. He emphasizes compassion as a guiding principle and defends a warrior's liberty to

Hojo Shigetoki's Warrior Ideal

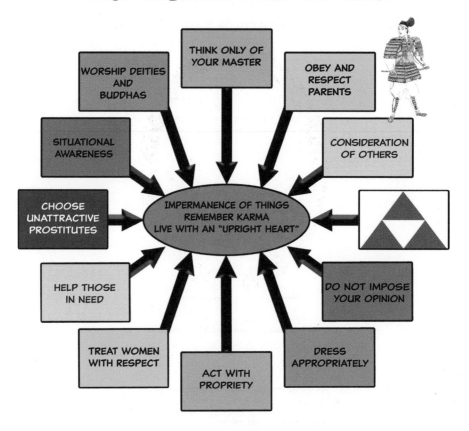

rule not just through military skill, although this was important, but by his efforts to nurture spiritual qualities and cultivate the mind. He urges his son to be a self-less, faithful servant to his lord, even if his dedication goes unnoticed. Perhaps symptomatic of his own aging, Shigetoki implores his son to have respect for his elderly parents, "For even though our faculties are fading and our behavior has become childlike, a similar fate awaits everyone." After all, the only thing a parent wants is for their son to be a good, upright man. If forthcoming advice is unwanted, sons must be grateful for the grace in which it is given.

A warrior chieftain will have to entertain guests and participate in gatherings. At such times, his first consideration is to ensure that others receive more food and drink. He should also avoid peering too intently when passing by a woman's living quarters and to instruct his subordinates to show the same restraint.

Speaking of women, a somewhat unanticipated injunction is to "choose ugly prostitutes," as any man is in danger of becoming besotted by a beauty and behaving in an excessive, unseemly manner. What is more, it is a sign of inferior breeding and arrogance to "speak ill of any woman irrespective of her station in life."

To push one's own opinion on others, no matter how reasonable one believes they are, will not be a cause of injury to the giver, but may well cause hardship or death to the receiver. Although it may seem harmless enough, "reason is not always right...." The warrior must be empathetic to the plight of others and rejoice in acts of compassion and spontaneous kindness. "This is good karma even if it is not immediately acknowledged." Moreover, the warrior is advised to "never speak badly of other men's foibles, and to always show respect to those of lower rank."

What is most regrettable is to treat favorably those deemed to be of value while ignoring others who are thought to be of little use. "A warrior who treats all with respect will himself be respected by his men and the gods."

Shiba Yoshimasa (1350–1410)
斯波義政

2. Polishing the Mind

Yoshimasa was the fourth son of Shiba Takatsune, a relation and staunch ally of Ashikaga Takauji. Yoshimasa wrote *Chikubasho* in 1368 during his second stint of three as deputy shogun (*kanrei*). He was rated highly as an administrator, military general, and poet, and exerted substantial influence in the Bakufu "as the voice of reason." *Chikubasho* is a single volume in which Yoshimasa urges his heirs to shine in both the military and the peaceful arts.

In the text there are minor references to Confucian teachings, but it generally reveals a much stronger Buddhist slant and offers practical and ethical advice to civilize the more violent tendencies of the warrior. He only mentions martial ability cursorily, as such matters go without saying. Instead, he accentuates the spiritual and cultural training necessary to govern with a "true mind" that acts on reason rather than emotion. In this sense, Yoshimasa was possibly the first warrior to write about cultivating the mind.

His wisdom notwithstanding, the Shiba clan descended into a bitter succession dispute in the mid-1400s, which contributed to the chaos of the Onin War. Eventually, their lands were confiscated by the Imagawa and Asakura clans, and in 1554 Oda Nobutomo hammered the last nail in the Shiba coffin by killing Shiba Yoshimune.

Shiba Yoshimasa's Warrior Ideal

竹馬抄   **BAMBOO STILT ANTHOLOGY**

DON'T HOLD LIFE TOO DEAR NOR TOO LIGHTLY

AVOID POINTLESS FIGHTS BUT BE PREPARED TO DIE FOR A WORTHY CAUSE

PLAN AHEAD

NEVER BE NEGLIGENT

LIFE

LOSE THE EGO

DON'T SEEK FAVOR BY SERVING. SERVE AND FAVOR COMES

BE READY FOR ANY CRISIS

IMITATE PARENT'S TEACHINGS RATHER THAN OTHERS EVEN IF THEY ARE FAULTY

SERVICE

SKILL IN THE ARTS BRINGS FAME AND HONOR

SKILL IN THE ARTS REQUIRES DISCIPLINE AND REFINEMENT

SKILL IN THE ARTS KEEPS YOU RELEVANT IN OLD AGE

HEART

ART

GREAT ARTISTS INFUSE THEIR HEARTS WITH THE MOON, FLOWERS, AND PURE INTENT

CALM AND ABLE TO SEE INTO THE MINDS OF OTHERS = BEST MARTIAL ART

USE THIS KNOWLEDGE = COMPASSION FOR THE BETTERMENT OF MANKIND

MAINTENANCE OF YOUR REPUTATION AND HONOR = That of both your ancestors and descendants

Writing during the contentious Nanbokucho era when two rival courts coexisted, Yoshimasa decreed that a warrior "must never hesitate to sacrifice his life for an important cause such as the defense of the emperor." He also reminded his heirs that their actions and reputation would have a lasting influence on their descendants. "The warrior must avoid staining his name for all time by desperately clinging to life." Conversely, he warns that disregard for the value of life and treating it as little more than "dust and ashes" to forfeit it at a time of no consequence is also detrimental to the clan's reputation.

Following one's "parents teachings even if they are flawed" is a curious principle, but was, in fact, an appeal to ensure that clan traditions are passed on. His attention to the arts, such as music and poetry, is not only for cultivating a vision for compassionate governance but, interestingly, to lay claim to skills that will be admired even when one is too old and decrepit to participate in war and administration. It is finesse in artistic pursuits, he asserts, that fosters cool-headedness to see into the hearts of others. This will, in turn, help you to utilize men in positions most suited to them, and is also the fundamental mindset in the military arts.

"Have he attitude to improve one step at a time, and take care in speech so as not to be thought a fool by others…." Furthermore, he cautioned, "Know that insincerity will lead to loss of control. All things should be fulfilled with singleness of mind…. Warriors must be composed and have the measure of others. This is the key to success in military matters." Honor and reputation are valued above all else. A man can achieve standing in society through knowledge in the arts and so should be schooled in them "regardless of whether he has ability or not…."

Imagawa Sadayo (1325–1420)
今川貞世

3. A Timeless Letter
Referred to as Ryoshun after he became a Buddhist priest in 1367, Imagawa Sadayo was a prominent general and strategist. His writings on military matters and ethics were to have a resonating effect on the professional outlook of Samurai for centuries to come. Although the shogun Ashikaga Yoshiakira made use of his military guile by dispatching him as his deputy to quell rebellions in problematic

regions such as Kyushu, he still found time to write on history, philosophy, and poetry. He was one of the most influential literary critics and poets of his time. Among his extensive body of work is the *Nan Taiheiki*, a critical look at historical errors contained in the *Taiheiki*. *Imagawa-jo* was a manual for his younger brother Nakaaki on how to conduct himself. It comprises twenty-three harsh observations of his brother's faults followed by another section in which Ryoshun softens the blow with kinder explanations of what he means.

This letter was first extolled as an ethical guidebook for the Imagawa clan but was destined to become a popular Samurai primer, and was even included in the Tokugawa shogunate's compendium of principal house codes compiled as reference material for the formulation of the regime's laws and procedures.

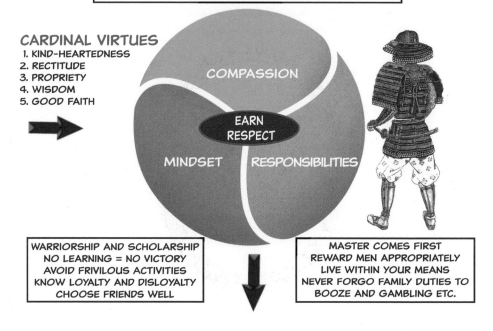

Imagawa Sadayo's Warrior Ideal

NO PASSING THE DEATH SENTENCE FOR MINOR CRIMES
NO EXPLOITATION OF THE PEOPLE FOR PERSONAL GAIN
REMEMBER DEBTS TO MASTER, ANCESTORS, AND PARENTS
DON'T CAUSE TROUBLE
NEVER RIDICULE OTHERS

CARDINAL VIRTUES
1. KIND-HEARTEDNESS
2. RECTITUDE
3. PROPRIETY
4. WISDOM
5. GOOD FAITH

COMPASSION

EARN RESPECT

MINDSET   RESPONSIBILITIES

WARRIORSHIP AND SCHOLARSHIP
NO LEARNING = NO VICTORY
AVOID FRIVILOUS ACTIVITIES
KNOW LOYALTY AND DISLOYALTY
CHOOSE FRIENDS WELL

MASTER COMES FIRST
REWARD MEN APPROPRIATELY
LIVE WITHIN YOUR MEANS
NEVER FORGO FAMILY DUTIES TO
BOOZE AND GAMBLING ETC.

EFFECTIVE MANAGEMENT OF SELF AND OTHERS
MAKES FOR A DISTINGUISHED WARRIOR

"It is natural for Samurai to learn the ways of war, and apply themselves to the acquisition of basic fighting skills. However, as is clearly stated in ancient military texts, without applying oneself to study [of the arts of peace], it is impossible to be a worthy ruler...." This is related to Ryoshun's first criticism of his brother, who apparently lacked the intellectual ability required of a leader.

Nakaaki was rebuked for his fondness for roaming around the countryside and engaging in frivolous diversions such as falconry and fishing when more serious matters needed attention. Hunting was an important activity in warrior training, but Ryoshun's warning is also related to the "purposeless taking of life." This is further highlighted in denunciations of Nakaaki's past deeds of putting petty criminals to death while showing favoritism to truly obnoxious individuals without discriminating between good or bad behavior in his men. "You reward them or punish them arbitrarily."

Nakaaki never readily accepted prudent advice. Instead, he bullied his advisors or used unreasonable force to get his own way. He was a gambler and drinker who neglected clan business, but still harbored delusions of his own cleverness. Ryoshun pulls no punches and finishes by beseeching Nakaaki to look into his own behavior with as much intensity as he does of others. "Realize that good and bad resides in your own mind. It is good when people of high and low station gather around you. If you are shunned, even though you plead with them to come, know that it is because of your own wickedness."

A negligent warrior lacking in wisdom, skill and training will be loathed by all. "A man of virtue looks for friends who are superior to he, and shies away from those who are not." The Samurai must therefore strive to accomplish everything to the best of his ability in civil and military matters without dropping his guard for a moment, and with the "five cardinal virtues firmly entrenched in his heart."

Ichijo Kaneyoshi (1402–81)
一条兼良

4. Relieve Suffering

Ichijo Kaneyoshi (aka Kanera) was the grandson of Nijo Yoshimoto and the son of Tsunetsugu, both imperial regents. He served as the grand minister of state in 1446 and became head of the Fujiwara family in 1447. Kaneyoshi authored works on traditional customs and practices, court rituals, politics, and religion. More than anything, he was a consummate poet, but is remembered mostly as a scholar of classical Japanese literature, such as the *Tale of Genji*.

Kaneyoshi was born in an age of prosperity for aristocrats. His lineage put him at the apex of court culture in Kyoto but the Onin War and the lawlessness that followed saw much of his effort on the maintenance of cultural mores and traditions laid to waste. He criticized the violence that engulfed his world, a sentiment that can be detected in the following ideas extracted from a letter he wrote to shogun Ashikaga Yoshinao (r. 1473–89).

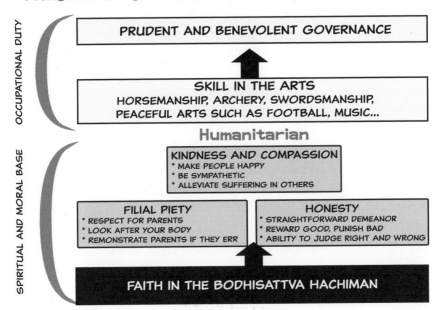

Ichijo Kaneyoshi's Ideal Warrior Leader

OCCUPATIONAL DUTY

PRUDENT AND BENEVOLENT GOVERNANCE

SKILL IN THE ARTS
HORSEMANSHIP, ARCHERY, SWORDSMANSHIP,
PEACEFUL ARTS SUCH AS FOOTBALL, MUSIC...

SPIRITUAL AND MORAL BASE

Humanitarian

KINDNESS AND COMPASSION
* MAKE PEOPLE HAPPY
* BE SYMPATHETIC
* ALLEVIATE SUFFERING IN OTHERS

FILIAL PIETY
* RESPECT FOR PARENTS
* LOOK AFTER YOUR BODY
* REMONSTRATE PARENTS IF THEY ERR

HONESTY
* STRAIGHTFORWARD DEMEANOR
* REWARD GOOD, PUNISH BAD
* ABILITY TO JUDGE RIGHT AND WRONG

FAITH IN THE BODHISATTVA HACHIMAN

"Acts of kindness are for alleviating suffering. Acts of compassion are for providing happiness. The wish to relieve suffering and deliver happiness is the heart of the Buddha. In Confucian teachings this sentiment is called humaneness, or the feeling of love towards other human beings. This is the same as kindness and compassion...."

Kaneyoshi laments the untold numbers of people from all stations in life who had been ripped from their homes and demoralized through starvation and bitter cold during the previous decade of strife. The people responsible for such thievery, he argues, are "bereft of kindness and compassion" and their wicked conduct will catch up with them eventually. "But their failure to know this is reprehensible." Vicious actions by men of once respectable and loyal clans brings disgrace to the memory of their ancestors. "Their villainous deeds will also be remembered for posterity and their descendants will suffer the consequences." As such, every aspect of governance must be just and carefully executed.

Of course, all work and no play makes Yoshinao a dull boy. Kaneyoshi encourages him to cultivate his artistic inclination and participate, within reason, in various cultural pursuits. Entertaining guests is also an occasion to be cherished, and exchanging cups of wine is enjoyable but not to the extent of becoming drunk and disorderly. "When you have imbibed enough to realize that you are intoxicated, and have lost sight of your basic nature, then it is time to retire. Myriad regrettable offences transpire without prudence at such times."

Kaneyoshi entreats Yoshinao to strengthen his faith in the deities and Buddhas and to do everything in his power to "make Japan great again." It is only through piety and a truly compassionate, kind, and humane outlook that success as a ruler is possible. This is also the primary basis of filial duty. Not looking after one's health, or not advising one's parents if they do wrong are also violations of filial duty. Attention to this is important because "Waiving such obligations to your parents will result in your own children doing the same to you."

When managing people, the wise ruler must know the difference between respectable and unruly men and treat them accordingly. This is the mark of a just government practiced with an honest mind. "An honest mind is just like a mirror. If a handsome person looks in a mirror, the reflection is stately. When an ugly person looks, the reflection is grotesque." Who is that peering in your mirror?

Kosaka Masanobu (1527–78)
高坂昌信

5. The Record of Kai

Kosaka Danjo Masanobu was a warrior who served the great warlords Takeda Shingen and his son Katsuyori. Masanobu has traditionally been credited with writing the *Koyo-gunkan* but its authorship is very much a matter of conjecture. Composed of twenty volumes and fifty-nine chapters, the prevalent theory was that the text was not only compiled in the early 1600s by Obata Kagenori, a renowned military scholar and teacher of Takeda military studies, but that the lion's share was probably written by him. Recently, however, scholars think that most of the content was in fact orated by Kosaka. The following section was most certainly a record of Kosaka's words.

Kosaka was born into a farming family but entered the service of Shingen at the age of sixteen, eventually rising up the ranks to become one of the legendary "Twenty-four Generals" in the Takeda army. The formidable Takedas were eventually decimated during Katsuyori's rule by Oda Nobunaga and his allies, first at the Battle of Nagashino in 1575, and then finally in 1582 at the Battle of Tenmokuzan. The book is believed to be an expression of Kosaka's grief as he witnessed the Takeda clan's sudden end following the rout at Nagashino.

Riddled with historical inaccuracies because of single-minded adulation of Takeda Shingen and perhaps Kosaka's fading memory, the book has long been considered an unreliable source. Nevertheless, there is an abundance of information about the trials and tribulations faced by Samurai during the Warring States period, and thus it became mandatory reading for Samurai of the Tokugawa shogunate. *Koyo-gunkan* influenced subsequent manuals addressing the peacetime warrior philosophy through the prominence of Obata's illustrious disciples such as Yamaga Soko and Daidoji Yuzan (see Chapter 4). *Koyo-gunkan* is often quoted in their works as communicating the essence of Bushido.

One of the more interesting chapters discusses four kinds of lords whose character traits ultimately lead to the destruction of their clans. It describes their shortcomings and the inevitable process of events that would unfold under their flawed tenure. The tone of *Koyo-gunkan* is unapologetic in its reverence of Shingen as an exemplary ruler, regarded as the benchmark for reference.

How did Shingen differ from other lords? The heart of the matter concerns "excess." A constant refrain throughout the *Koyo-gunkan* is the assertion that balance is critical and extremes are to be avoided at all costs. The book is thus full of examples on the maintenance of equilibrium in a variety of situations. From military strategy and everyday living to the character of a military leader, these examples take the form of admonitions: "Taken to excess, this is what will happen...."

Also contained within its volumes is the "Heiho Okigusho." Attributed to the legendary Takeda general Yamamoto Kansuke, this document is reputedly one of Japan's earliest martial art essays offering practical instruction in sword work, spear fighting, gunmanship, and archery. Of particular interest here, *Koyo-gunkan* is believed to be the first book to ever use the word *bushido*.

The "Myogo" volume in *Koyo-gunkan* is named after an oxen with a bladed tail. According to legend, the ox licks its tail because it takes delight in the sweet taste of its own blood. However, if it indulges too much, its tongue will become shredded and the ox will bleed to death. Kosaka compares this behavior to the behavior of the four kinds of flawed lords ("foolish lord," "the lord who is too clever," "the cowardly lord," and "the lord who is too strong"). All of these behaviors cause the destruction of their family lines and domains.

Baka Naru Taisho

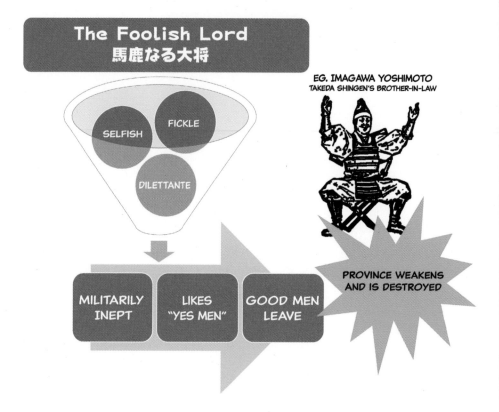

The Foolish Lord
馬鹿なる大将

SELFISH FICKLE

DILETTANTE

MILITARILY INEPT LIKES "YES MEN" GOOD MEN LEAVE

EG. IMAGAWA YOSHIMOTO
TAKEDA SHINGEN'S BROTHER-IN-LAW

PROVINCE WEAKENS AND IS DESTROYED

6. Supreme Numskull

First, the foolish lord, also referred to as doltish, silly, or stupid, lacks common sense and is for the most part conceited and selfish. He is obsessed with excursions, sightseeing, moon watching, flower viewing, poetry, linked verse, Noh, and the performing arts. As far as the martial arts are concerned, although he sometimes receives instruction in archery, swordsmanship, horse riding, and firearms, "his benighted frame of mind means he cannot devote himself to mastering the most basic skills, and ends up going through the motions as if it were merely a performance."

He flatters himself as being a "great lord." He thinks that everything he does is "exceptionally good." His sycophantic retainers continue to sing his praises, and as many as nine out of ten of his men will curry favor while behaving inappropriately. "There are many bad men in his coterie. This is only natural as everything the foolish lord does negates reason." Wicked retainers rise and so others either imitate them or quit their posts.

Rikon Sugitaru Taisho

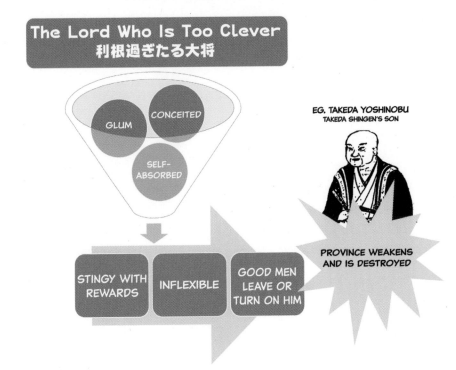

The Lord Who Is Too Clever
利根過ぎたる大将

GLUM

CONCEITED

SELF-ABSORBED

STINGY WITH REWARDS

INFLEXIBLE

GOOD MEN LEAVE OR TURN ON HIM

EG. TAKEDA YOSHINOBU
TAKEDA SHINGEN'S SON

PROVINCE WEAKENS AND IS DESTROYED

7. Dimly Bright

Second is the lord who is too clever. This kind of lord is generally vulgar, rude, and conceited. He is also downcast when things do not go his way. "An excellent Samurai whether of high or low rank will not become arrogant when matters are proceeding to plan, and does not become disheartened when smitten with bad luck." This is because he is wise and gallant. An inconsiderate lord, such as the one who is "too clever," lacks discretion and is actually a fool. He is destined to regularly fail in his responsibilities. Above all, the lord who is too clever "harbors many impish desires, and he chooses second-rate plots of land to give his retainers when allocating fiefs. The lord who is too clever will say things with an air of authority, but his true meaning is callous and vile."

The lord who is too clever will be haughty and thinks that "anything he does is above reproach." He takes no notice of past teachings of wise men, believing that his way is the only way. "Sometimes he may call for a learned monk to consult on a specific subject, or will read some texts. Forever convinced of his own cleverness, however, he will proclaim to have understood all after listening to only a little. He will interpret the words of a wise man in accordance with his own wicked desires."

The lord who is too clever is crude and "ranks sex above all else." If victorious in battle, he will inevitably be far away from the action. "In spite of this, he will tell tall tales of how he crushed the enemy single-handedly. He will be jealous of his own brave retainers, and afraid that his lies will be discovered, he may even expel them or have them killed."

8. Chicken Heart

Third, the cowardly lord (the lord who is too weak) "is constantly moaning like a woman." He is envious of wealthy people and prefers subordinates who curry favor with him. "Being unobservant, imprudent, uncompassionate, and inconsiderate, he is a terrible judge of character." The cowardly lord is stubborn and cruel and squanders his time mired in indecision. Having a heart full of foolishness, everyone views him as effeminate stooge. "Even with twenty or thirty thousand, or fifty or sixty thousand men, there will not even be a hundred who appreciate him."

Okubyo Naru Taisho

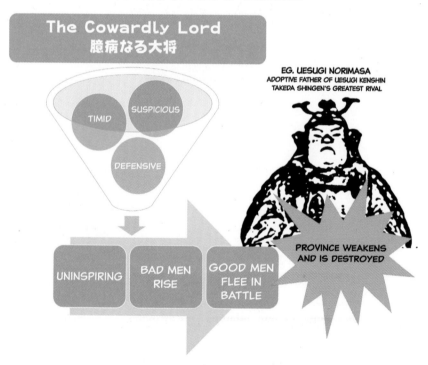

The Cowardly Lord
臆病なる大将

TIMID
SUSPICIOUS
DEFENSIVE

UNINSPIRING
BAD MEN RISE
GOOD MEN FLEE IN BATTLE

EG. UESUGI NORIMASA
ADOPTIVE FATHER OF UESUGI KENSHIN
TAKEDA SHINGEN'S GREATEST RIVAL

PROVINCE WEAKENS
AND IS DESTROYED

Such a narrow-minded, incompetent lord acts as if he were accomplished but does not know how to discern which of his men are good or bad, and indiscriminately hands out stipends, fiefs, money, and rice. "He is especially slow at making up his mind, so things go round in circles with little being accomplished...."

A cowardly lord ignores his obligations and seeks only to enhance his reputation. "He thinks about the present and not the future. He pampers his supporters without determining whether they are truly loyal and brave or cowardly, and passively agrees with what the majority says is good." In this way, it is difficult to discriminate between what is meritorious behavior and what is not, and so his retainers lose their drive to be daring and fearless.

9. Inordinately Able

The fourth flawed lord is the one who is "too strong." He is bold, astute, eloquent, and persuasive. He is wiser than other men and despises any form of weakness. He never loses his temper and is at no time irrational, so one would assume that he was an ideal lord.

This is not true. "When a House Elder is in a position to offer some advice, he thinks that such a triviality will put his lord in a foul mood; so out of ten issues, he will only mention five, and even then three issues will not be broached adequately."

Tsuyo Sugitaru Taisho

The Lord Who Is Too Strong
強過ぎたる大将

ELOQUENT
BRAVE
DESPISES WEAKNESS

EG. TAKEDA KATSUYORI
TAKEDA SHINGEN'S SON AND HEIR

MEN HOLD BACK
BRAGGARTS RISE
TRIES TO SURPASS ANCESTORS

PROVINCE WEAKENS AND IS DESTROYED

The "strong" the lord will therefore start to think that advice from his House Elders is hardly worth listening to, and as a result he becomes absorbed in his own ideas. "As the father of such a lord happens to have been famous, he will reluctantly meet with the old House Elders. They will engage in various discussions, but under such a headstrong young master, their guidance is futile."

Out of desperation, they say whatever comes into their heads "and contrive all manner of inoperative proposals without thinking the consequences through." Meddling Samurai see opportunities for a change of guard and try to catch their lord's eye for promotion to House Elder, although their advice has no substance.

Furthermore, a lord who is too strong will always be in high spirits, but this will be his downfall. Battles that should not have been engaged in will result in needless casualties and crucial encounters will be lost with many good men perishing in the process. "If good men die, 'apish' Samurai will tarry, and overall conduct in the ranks will deteriorate." If his military clout unravels this way, the lord will, conversely, earn a reputation for weakness. "Thus a lord who was too strong will be consigned to history as being no different to the weak lords...."

Kosaka considered competence to discern the qualities of one's men, the aptitude to instantaneously judge situations, and being benevolent in character as basic traits necessary in the consummate warlord. A good warlord was able to rouse his men into performing deeds of merit in battle and he was certain to reward them appropriately.

He also stresses that the quality of the lord dictates the quality of his subordinates. "Generally, a Samurai of lowly rank who is a buffoon, is so because his lord is a dunderhead.... An ox will follow an ox, and a horse will follow a horse." Survival of the clan depended on the caliber of its leader. The warlord needed to be a role model to his men in order to carry the day. In the course of the Tokugawa period, such precedents were grafted onto the commission of rank-and-file Samurai who had become privileged custodians of their communities.

不動如山　侵掠如火　其徐如林　其疾如風

The Takeda Clan's motto. "Be as rapid as the wind, as gentle as a forest, as vigorous as fire in attack, and as immovable as a mountain."

Chapter 4

Tokugawa Samurai Ideals
徳川時代の武士思想

As Japan fought its way through the tumultuous Warring States period in the late 15th and 16th centuries, warrior ethics reflected a world of extreme violence. Death was not an abstract ideal but a reality. With the establishment of the Tokugawa shogunate early in the 17th century, the country was finally ushered into an era of cautious peace after more than a century and a half of turmoil. The Samurai ideal founded on day-to-day intimacy with death and unbridled brutality was no longer in harmony with the times. Men-of-war were now called upon to fill administrative positions in the organs of provincial and central government.

Although not as prosperous as affluent townsmen who were taking advantage of the flourishing economy, those born to Samurai status occupied the upper echelon of society, allowing them to lord it over farmers, artisans, merchants, and outcasts. Despite this, justification for warrior authority in the Tokugawa period was questioned, not by their social inferiors but by the Samurai themselves. A new kind of "Edo Bushido" was the order of the day, an ideology that valued the customs and spirit of the warriors of yesteryear but was more conducive to the standards of friendly relations promoted by the Tokugawa. The mind of the warrior and his credibility needed refocusing. The Samurai needed domesticating.

Warrior ideals matured throughout the Tokugawa period but with considerable regional variation. For the sake of convenience, however, scholars in Japan broadly divide the early modern warrior honor code into two types. The first was the provincial Samurai psyche represented by classic treatises such as *Hagakure*. It demanded uncompromising loyalty to the domain lord and was typically unabashedly region-centric. Depending on how far the province was located from Edo, it could even be tinged with seditious anti-shogunate sentiment. I refer to it as hard-core "bull-headed Bushido."

The other kind, represented by texts such as *Budo Shoshinshu*, was a fusion of Confucian and military studies and emphasized appropriate law-abiding conduct for all Samurai rather than just members of a given clan. The duties of the Samurai were spelled out unambiguously in the form of "how to" manuals, and although death remained a primary consideration, maintenance of social order adhering to Confucian precepts was the overarching theme. I call this soft-core "balmy (temperate) Bushido."

Sagara Toru, an eminent scholar on Samurai ethics and thought, loosely categorized these two modes of Samurai dogma as "Hagakure Bushido" and "Confucian Bushido." They make for an interesting study of contrasts but also have much in common. At their root was an acceptance of and preparedness for death. Always central to the warrior ethos, death was to become even more idealized during the Tokugawa period as the reality and memory of war faded. This chapter will outline some of the most representative examples of Tokugawa period Samurai ideals.

Nakae Toju (1608–48)
中江藤樹

1. Coexistence of War and Culture

Nakae Toju was the founder of the Wang Yangming school of Confucianism (Yomeigaku) in Japan. Born a farmer's son in Omi (present-day Shiga Prefecture), he left home at the age of nine to study under his grandfather, a retainer to the lord in the province of Iyo (Ehime Prefecture). Upon completing his studies, he returned to his birthplace and opened a private school where he taught Confucian philosophy. His reputation as an outstanding human being and scholar earned him the moniker the "Sage of Omi."

Although Toju started with the Neo-Confucian philosophy of Zhu Xi, in his mid-thirties he converted to the Wang Yangming school. The difference between the two philosophies is that in the Zhu Xi school, *ri* (the principle of universal reason) originates from a "Supreme Ultimate" (*taikyoku*), whereas Wang Yangming taught that *ri* is to be found in the individual's mind and is known instinctively. Therefore, Toju instructed the importance of moral conduct emanating from within and of the indispensable weight of justice in action and thought, that is, to be your own master and live in a morally upright way. To this end, Toju maintained that action and thought must be in harmony and that integrity surpassed intellect. This line of reasoning influenced many prominent thinkers, including Kumazawa Banzan, who were proactive on bringing about social change in place of blind social conformity.

Nakae Toju's Confucian Warrior Ideal

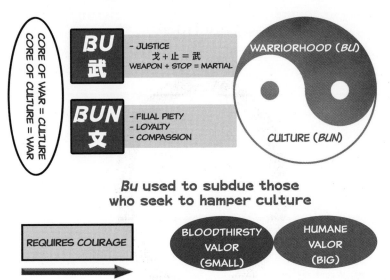

Toju's theories provided Samurai with "the moral foundation for political action." His *Okina mondo* (Dialogues with an Old Man, 1641) is his best-known work. According to Toju's ideals, martial (*bu*) and cultural (*bun*) affairs were essentially a unified entity. Therefore, culture was not complete without warriorhood and warriorhood was not complete without culture. He was not inciting war. The ideogram for *bu* (武), he deliberated, suggests that the true meaning for martial is to "stop violence," not to "stop *with* violence." In other words, the objective of the warrior was to serve in the name of culture. A cultured mind was required to keep the peace but a firm hand was sometimes permissible if all else failed. As such, he argued that the essence of culture was inextricably and paradoxically linked with warriorhood.

Culture represented compassion whereas warriorhood represented rectitude or justice. The virtues of compassion and rectitude are two wheels of a cart that cannot be separated. "As compassion is the virtue that represents culture, it forms the basis of peaceful arts such as poetry, music and the like. Justice is the virtue of warriorhood. It is the seed of the martial arts and sciences, such as swordsmanship and strategy. Without these two virtues at their core, both the cultural and martial arts are bereft of genuine value."

If the warrior has a compassionate and just mind in his resolution to perfect the cultural and military arts, "he will be imbued with a demeanor that is refined and kind in normal times, but will be a demon in battle." This is what Toju called "concealed courage."

Courage is mandatory to quell those who would disturb the peace and bring culture to ruin. To subdue enemies of culture with a predilection for violence and bloodshed is beastly, inferior, murderous valor. It lacks reason and is unjust. "To fight as a last resort with humaneness as the defender of justice and culture is the superior way."

"The warrior must strive to be conscientious; a person whom others can respect and trust. He must observe the 'Five Moral Behaviors' and be a man of unimpeachable character." To redress the hearts of others, he must first straighten his mind.

A government that rules with fairness and integrity evinces the moral incorruptibility of its leaders. A government that rules by the letter of the law is symptomatic of a lack of principled fortitude. Thus, they need the law to launder their own hypocritical stances. "A government of upstanding moral fiber is the guardant of culture. The leader must be sagacious in exercising his convictions for the benefit of all."

Body and Soul of the Samurai

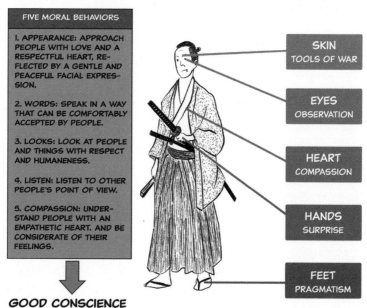

FIVE MORAL BEHAVIORS

1. APPEARANCE: APPROACH PEOPLE WITH LOVE AND A RESPECTFUL HEART, REFLECTED BY A GENTLE AND PEACEFUL FACIAL EXPRESSION.

2. WORDS: SPEAK IN A WAY THAT CAN BE COMFORTABLY ACCEPTED BY PEOPLE.

3. LOOKS: LOOK AT PEOPLE AND THINGS WITH RESPECT AND HUMANENESS.

4. LISTEN: LISTEN TO OTHER PEOPLE'S POINT OF VIEW.

5. COMPASSION: UNDERSTAND PEOPLE WITH AN EMPATHETIC HEART. AND BE CONSIDERATE OF THEIR FEELINGS.

GOOD CONSCIENCE

SKIN
TOOLS OF WAR

EYES
OBSERVATION

HEART
COMPASSION

HANDS
SURPRISE

FEET
PRAGMATISM

Toju Nakae, *New World Encyclopedia.*

Toju equated the military arts with the human body. Naturally, compassion represents the heart, powers of perception and observation are the eyes, pragmatism and surprise are defined by the hands and feet, and the skin and hair are logistics. "Procuring and using the weapons of war were the skin and hair." The problem, he observed, is that "most people think of the skin and hair as the cornerstone of the martial arts and military science. There is so much more required to prevail in battle."

"The eyes must be unclouded and the feet and hands trained and deft. A truly admirable warrior is proficient in all of these things, but is steadied by a heart that is humane and scrupulous." For this purpose, it was important for the Samurai to "nurture his mind by immersing it in culture and the peaceful arts before dousing himself into the military arts and tempering the eyes, hands and feet." It is the humane and the just who prevail in the end.

Hojo Ujinaga (1600–70)
北条氏長

2. Reinterpreting the Warrior's Role

Hojo Ujinaga studied the Koshu-ryu school of military strategy under Obata Kagenori (1572–1663). With the coveted rank of *hatamoto* (bannerman) in the Tokugawa shogunate, Ujinaga held several influential posts in the government, including chief inspector (*ometsuke*) for Iemitsu, the third Tokugawa shogun.

Ujinaga expanded the principles of leadership he learned from Kagenori. Sidestepping some of the more esoteric methods described in previous military studies, he steered his doctrine towards a rational political approach.

Tokugawa shoguns Iemitsu and Ietsuna took counsel from him, as did many *daimyo* lords throughout the country. In addition to these illustrious patrons, he also trained a generation of scholars, such as Yamaga Soko and Daidoji Yuzan, who would later become acclaimed authorities in the field of Samurai ethics.

Ujinaga's *Shikan Yoho* (1646) became the main textbook for his teachings and remained an influential work long after his death. In it, he reinterprets classics such as Sun-tzu's *Art of War* to complement Japan's new political and cultural setting. "Soldiers are the most important part of the state, the basis of life and death, the Way to survival or extinction. Their role must be thoroughly pondered and analyzed."

In other words, the condition of the country's warriors was an indication of the health of the realm. As such, "it is incumbent on Samurai to seek perfection in all their affairs, treating life as a proxy for the battlefield, as they protect the prosperity of their principality and the perpetuation of peace."

Hojo Ujinaga's Warrior Ideal

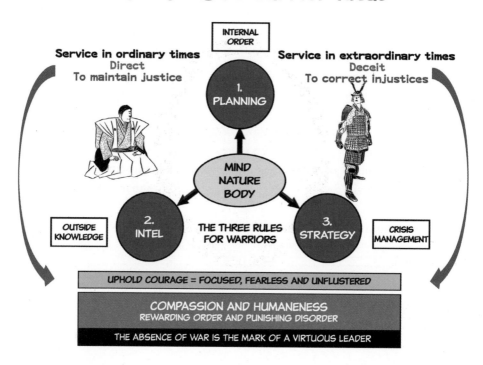

According to Ujinaga, "the Way of the Samurai is centered on military affairs, *bu*. The implementation of reason for governance is civil rule or *bun*. Meting out punishments to keep people in line is *bu*, and is for keeping the masses orderly and productive."

Guiding the realm in times of peace required directness while also rewarding virtuous deeds to inspire respectful behavior. Wresting control from evildoers in times of upheaval required a transition to military rule. Ensuring victory over evil through cunning and devious means was acceptable as per the rules of military strategy. "Subterfuge or deceit is reserved for reprimanding sinister malefactors, but is never to be used against allies." The superior warrior was one whose leadership enabled freedom from civil disturbance. The fact that there was no war was not to be lamented "but seen as proof of the ruler's excellence."

"There are three rules that the Samurai is obliged to uphold: operative planning (internal order), obtaining intelligence (knowing the outside world), and mastery of strategic procedures (contingency plans for emergencies)." The Samurai, argues Ujinaga, "must always train his mind and body to remain calm and composed, and to never succumb to emotional sentiments or desires." In an age when it was easy to become self-satisfied through blissful unawareness of dangers or deficiencies, this required vigilance and courage, never taking anything for granted.

Ujinaga declares that the four classes of people (Samurai, farmers, artisans, and merchants) all have important roles to play. "Those who cultivate food are the farmers. Artisans craft items necessary for everyday living. It is the merchants who deliver tools to the farmers, food to the artisans, and sell everybody's produce."

What of the Samurai? What function do they have in the workings of society? "As long as the lord acts in concord with universal principles, and he and his men conform to a standard of what is right and good, ever mindful of their deportment as they willingly perform their designated duties, then the farmers, artisans, and merchants will prosper."

For the Samurai, restraint was of the essence. Should warriors adopt bad ways and let the "Ten Extremes" contaminate their behavior, all will suffer and the country will be destined for ruin. Therefore, precisely because it was peacetime, Samurai were seen by Ujinaga as being the most important constituent of the realm. It was their behavior that guaranteed the continued security or the eventual decay of society.

The Ten Extremes to Be Avoided

COURAGE	EXTREME = ONE TAKES LIFE LIGHTLY
SWIFTNESS	EXTREME = ONE BECOMES IMPULSIVE
POVERTY	EXTREME = ONE DESIRES PROFIT
BENEVOLENCE	EXTREME = ONE IS NOT RESOLUTE WITH OTHERS
KNOWLEDGE	EXTREME = ONE BECOMES AFRAID OF THE UNKNOWN
TRUST	EXTREME = ONE BLINDLY TRUSTS OTHERS
PROPRIETY	EXTREME = ONE LACKS EMPATHY
WISDOM	EXTREME = ONE BECOMES COMPLACENT
STRENGTH	EXTREME = ONE BECOMES TOO INDEPENDENT
NEED	EXTREME = ONE LEAVES THINGS TO OTHERS

Kumazawa Banzan (1619–91)
熊沢蕃山

3. Reconciling War with Compassion

A pre-eminent Confucian scholar, Kumazawa Banzan was the eldest son of six children of a masterless Samurai (*ronin*) in Kyoto. When he was eight, he was adopted by his grandfather who served the Tokugawa *daimyo* of Mito. Banzan was later employed for a short period of five years by the *daimyo* Ikeda Mitsumasa of Bizen (Okayama Prefecture) in 1634.

After resigning his post, he studied under the founder of the Wang Yangming school of Confucianism in Japan, Nakae Toju. Banzan excelled in his training to become Toju's star student. Brimming with knowledge and an unshakable social conscience, Banzan returned to Bizen in 1645 and served under Mitsumasa once again. He had more influence in the domain's administration now and instigated significant agricultural, economic, and educational reforms before being promoted to the domain's full-time professor in 1656. He was very much an advocate of a political system based on merit rather than birthright. Being a somewhat radical reformer, he locked horns with traditionalists and even the shogunate itself and was forced into retirement as a result.

Banzan produced much of his work after this time. Considered to be among his most revelatory are two compendiums of dialogues and letters. The first is *Shugi Washo*, which explores morality, and the second is *Shugi Gaisho*, which addresses political and social issues.

He also wrote *Daigaku Wakumon* (Questions on the Great Learning) in which he expounds on subjects ranging from military strategy to economic management, as well as the Confucian classics and indigenous Japanese literature. He was revered by later notable Samurai such as Yoshida Shoin and Katsu Kaishu, who praised him as a "hero of the people." The following synopsis of Banzan's ideal warrior is taken from *Shugi Washo*.

Wisdom (*chi*), benevolence (*jin*), and valor (*yu*) are virtues in both the martial (*bu*) and literary (*bun*) arts. "From the literary arts, the warrior learns compassion. From the military arts he understands the meaning of justice." Nevertheless, according to Banzan's reasoning, to refer to the archetypical warrior as someone who is accomplished in both the "Ways" of *bu* and *bun* is a misnomer. Although literary and military pursuits are both arts, they cannot be referred to as "Ways" if the dilettante lacks wisdom, benevolence, and valor. Thus, first and foremost, it is "these three virtues that form the bedrock of the warrior's path."

The ideal warrior should be literate and keen on learning. If he is not this way inclined, the least he can do is focus on his duty as a warrior and always be eager to earn a reputation for fortitude and honor rather than fritter away in his comfort zone.

That said, it is not virtuous to "hope for the rise of conflict for a chance to shine." Too many people suffer needlessly in times of war. Likewise, it is inappropriate to yearn for peace simply because it is less stressful. "The warrior is duty-bound to be primed and ready for anything." This tempered by the warning "He must never openly boast of his courage and strength as this will work against him. Nobody likes a braggart, and good deeds will go unacknowledged."

Devotion to the Warrior's Way

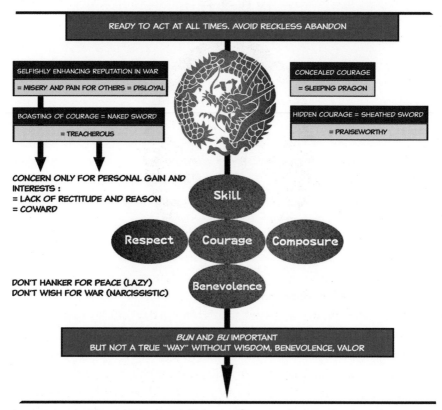

READY TO ACT AT ALL TIMES. AVOID RECKLESS ABANDON

SELFISHLY ENHANCING REPUTATION IN WAR
= MISERY AND PAIN FOR OTHERS = DISLOYAL

CONCEALED COURAGE
= SLEEPING DRAGON

BOASTING OF COURAGE = NAKED SWORD
= TREACHEROUS

HIDDEN COURAGE = SHEATHED SWORD
= PRAISEWORTHY

CONCERN ONLY FOR PERSONAL GAIN AND INTERESTS :
= LACK OF RECTITUDE AND REASON
= COWARD

Skill

Respect   Courage   Composure

DON'T HANKER FOR PEACE (LAZY)
DON'T WISH FOR WAR (NARCISSISTIC)

Benevolence

BUN AND BU IMPORTANT
BUT NOT A TRUE "WAY" WITHOUT WISDOM, BENEVOLENCE, VALOR

Ultimate Warrior's Way = Compassion and Respect

MAXIMUM EFFICIENCY, MAXIMUM LOYALTY, MAXIMUM EMPATHY

Similarly, a man who thinks only of personal gain and puts on airs lacks the qualities of someone with a fair and reasonable mind. "He will be scorned as a poltroon [coward] deficient in the most fundamental human qualities." In his heart of hearts, the warrior has courage—concealed courage—that is, latent energy that can explode into action like a sleeping dragon. "Until that time, the warrior must personify the virtues of loving compassion and respect for all people."

Yamaga Soko (1622–85)
山鹿素行

4. Shido and Dedication to Duty

Yamaga Soko was a highly successful scholar in his day and his impact on the redefinition of the Samurai code was far-reaching. His students included *daimyo* lords and thousands of Samurai of all ranks. His popularity can be attributed to the succinct answers he had to the many dilemmas warriors faced in peacetime. He was able to express his opinions in a way that could be readily understood.

In many ways, Soko helped Samurai justify their existence in an age without war. This was helpful not only for the rank-and-file Samurai but also for the Tokugawa government whose primary concern was maintaining social stability.

Of his many works, *Bukyo-shogaku* was a short book consisting of ten sections outlining the obligatory tasks of a Samurai when the nation was not at war. Authored in the same tone as a Confucian primer for children, it was a simple text that joined the dots on how to behave as a man worthy of his social status. After all, a Samurai did not make or produce anything, so how could he justify the stipend he received off the backs of hardworking commoners. Soko's answer was that because a Samurai was engaged in the service of his lord, and because he ranked above the ordinary people, his moral duty was to keep up appearances, behave appropriately, and become a role model worthy of admiration and emulation.

"This comes to pass by simply getting out of bed early in the morning, washing one's face, arranging one's hair, adjusting one's attire, and taking up one's swords." Then the Samurai composed himself, recalling the benevolence of both his father and his lord, before planning the day's activities. Living the "right way" as such was precisely the Way of the warrior, or *shido* as Soko referred to it.

Yamaga Soko's Shido

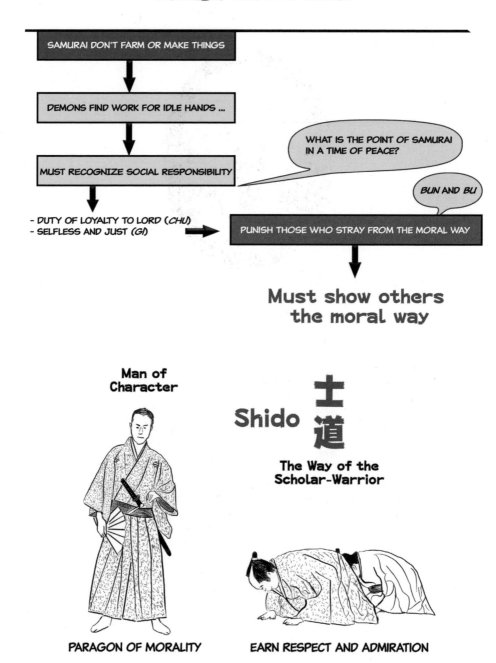

SAMURAI DON'T FARM OR MAKE THINGS

DEMONS FIND WORK FOR IDLE HANDS ...

MUST RECOGNIZE SOCIAL RESPONSIBILITY

- DUTY OF LOYALTY TO LORD (*CHU*)
- SELFLESS AND JUST (*GI*)

WHAT IS THE POINT OF SAMURAI IN A TIME OF PEACE?

BUN AND *BU*

PUNISH THOSE WHO STRAY FROM THE MORAL WAY

Must show others the moral way

Man of Character

Shido 士道

The Way of the Scholar-Warrior

PARAGON OF MORALITY

EARN RESPECT AND ADMIRATION

The Samurai does not involve himself with the business of farmers, artisans, and merchants. Instead, he devotes himself to practicing the Way of the "superior man." Should someone in the other three classes of common people behave immorally, it was the Samurai's duty to see that the transgressor was punished. He was the enforcer of correct human conduct.

To this end, it was unthinkable for a Samurai to know martial and civil virtues without actually demonstrating them in his own behavior. "He must be ready for action should the call come for military assistance. This is why he must practice the military arts." At the same time, "He occupies his war-less days travailing to meet the requirements of the Confucian Way of 'lord and subject,' 'friend and friend,' 'father and son,' 'older and younger brother,' and 'husband and wife'."

He is ready for battle on the outside but on the inside he desires peace. "The common people look upon him as their teacher. They respect him as morally irreproachable. Through his words and actions they learn the difference between right and wrong." This was the Samurai's commission. It was how he repaid his obligations to his lord and the people and justified his food, clothing, and shelter.

Kaibara Ekken (1630–1714)
貝原益軒

5. War is Evil

Kaibara Ekken (Ekiken) was a Confucian scholar born into a Samurai family of the Fukuoka domain. He served under Kuroda Tadayuki but was stripped of his position and stipends in 1649 following an altercation with his lord. As a *ronin*, he traveled to Nagasaki to study the Western sciences of medicine and botany from Dutch traders.

Ekken returned to the Fukuoka domain in 1656 and was restored to his former position by Kuroda Mitsuyuki. He spent the rest of his career there and wrote several volumes on Confucian philosophy and natural sciences. His best-known works include *Yamato Honzo* (The Book of Life-nourishing Principles, 1708), which catalogues over 1,300 medicinal herbs, and *Yojokun*, which offers advice on health and well-being. His works interlace Confucian ethics with Japanese culture in the form of self-help books promoting moral cultivation and order.

The following outline of Ekken's interpretation of the Way of the warrior is from his well-known exposition called "Bukun" (Martial Precepts). This was part of a set titled *Bunbukun* (Literary and Martial Precepts) discovered in an 1893 collation of his work, *Ekken Jukkun*.

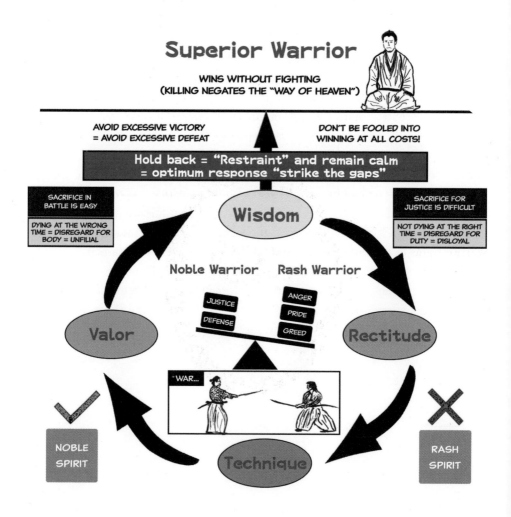

Any Samurai can offer his life in combat if he has an uncontrollable thirst for blood, but to fight and die for a truly just cause takes a different kind of courage and conviction. "To sacrifice oneself recklessly lacks compassion and amounts to a gross disregard of the precious life bestowed upon one by one's parents." Avoiding death when it is time to stake your life on a righteous cause, however, is also an act of disloyalty. "War contravenes the natural laws of the universe and should be avoided wherever possible. Fighting for justice or in self-defense is permissible, but still, a consummate warrior never kills more than he needs to."

War waged out of anger, pride, or greed is wrong and cannot be justified. Before engaging in conflict, the warrior needs insight and knowledge, a sense of honesty and correct moral behavior, ability in martial techniques and strategy, and physical fortitude to face death. Right-minded precedents are mandatory in war, and it must be "conducted wisely and honorably." Derogatory behavior toward one's enemies was considered crass and not the mark of the true hero. "Discretion is the key in war as it was proof of perceptiveness and compassion."

Waiting for the optimum time to strike with maximum efficiency while restricting the number of casualties in both enemy and allied camps was the mark of a first-rate man-at-arms. "The Samurai should never jump in rashly and make the first move of aggression." It was also important, Ekken advocated, to deal with people in everyday life, even if they are ignorant fools, "with forbearance and politeness to avoid conflict altogether." "Killing is cold and inhumane," he continues, "but to let evil burgeon is also a blight to justice." Warriors were to be cultured gentlemen, not thugs, who must assess any situation with great wisdom and discernment. "Without prudence and humanity the very things for which the warrior fights to uphold—culture and civility—can never be sustained."

"Military science" (*heiho*) is the "root" of martial arts. Therefore, "only studying martial techniques such as swordsmanship, archery and the like without understanding the scientific or theoretical principles underlying them, makes the military arts simple diversions with no substance."

Martial Arts (Individual Combat)

MILITARY ARTS

HALBERD

SWORDSMANSHIP

GUNMANSHIP

ARCHERY

SWIMMING

STAFF

SPEARMANSHIP

GRAPPLING

WARRIOR'S WAY

LITERARY ARTS (MARTIAL VIRTUE)
COMPASSION, RECTITUDE,
LOYALTY, HONESTY, FAITH, PIETY...
DIFFERENCE BETWEEN WARRIOR AND BANDIT

"The martial arts are for individual combat, but military science forms the basis for tactics on both large and small scales, and is thus a cruciform element in the warrior's education." Beneath military science are the Confucian virtues of loyalty, reason, filial piety, and integrity. "These qualities must define the warrior's heart before he begins to wield his weapons, lest he degenerate into a violent beast with no modicum of humanity." The warrior must therefore also study the literary arts to nurture a mind that is merciful and fair. This is what is meant by the term *butoku* (martial virtue). "Without martial virtue, there can be no warrior's Way."

Naganuma Tansai (1635–90)
長沼澹斎

6. War is Justifiable, Sometimes

Son of a Samurai serving the Matsumoto clan in Shinano, one of my favorite
Bushïdo commentators, Naganuma Tansai, founded the Naganuma-ryu school
of military tactics. Studying the Chinese classics under a learned monk, Muneyoshi joined the ranks of the Kano clan in 1652. He left in 1656 aged twenty-two
and made his way to Edo to further his education. Finding employment with
Arima Yoritoshi, lord of the Kurume domain, he wrote two notable books on
military training and combat application: *Heiyo-roku* and *Akuki Hachijin-shuke*.
These became textbooks for the Naganuma-ryu, which he taught to Samurai of
all ranks in the Kurume domain.

In 1682, Matsudaira Naoakira of the Akashi clan invited Tansai to serve as a
counselor, but he declined in order to take care of his ailing mother. Other lords
subsequently reached out to him in the hope that he would tutor their warriors,
but he refused all offers to live the rest of his life as a recluse in Fushimi (Kyoto).

Justification of Conflict

Yang = Fire = Threaten   Yin = Water = Compassion

* DISPATCHING BANDITS
* KILLING TYRANTS
* STOPPING CORRUPTION
* QUASHING TREASON
* SLAYING AGITATORS
* SMASHING OPPORTUNISTS
* STOPPING WARMONGERS

JUST WAR

CULTIVATE LIFE, RESTORE ORDER, PREVENT WRONGDOING

Although a cardinal expert in military matters, Tansai's view of warfare had a decidedly pacifist leaning. War to Tansai was a last resort to preserve order in the land. He detested combative people who encouraged unethical conflict to satisfy their bloodthirsty cravings and those who justified violence for personal gain.

Tansai identifies seven instances when war is acceptable: 1. To quash a tyrannical government creating hardship and suffering among the people; 2. To kill agitators seeking to upset harmony in an otherwise peaceful domain; 3. To punish treasonous senior officials who usurp power from their lord; 4. To prevent the domain from collapsing through the nepotistic schemes of corrupt officials operating under a weak lord; 5. To prevent disloyal opportunists from taking advantage of unruliness to bolster their own fortunes when the central government is in disarray; 6. To block warmongers who enlist allies to settle generation-old grudges; 7. To kill bandits who run riot when the country is in a state of anarchy.

Naganuma Tansai's Warrior Ideal

文 **Bun** CIVIC VIRTUE 知 **Chi** INTELLIGENCE 武 **Bu** MARTIAL VIRTUE

信 **Shin** FAITH

仁 Compassion
礼 Propriety
誠 *Makoto* SINCERITY
義 Duty
勇 Courage

SURIVIAL

Only when war is the sole recourse to mitigate disaster and rid the world of harm is it warranted. This is a "reactive" war where there is little choice. The opposite is "predacious" war motivated by a selfish and excessive desire for glory and power.

"Fire," he states "represents the threatening force keeping menaces at bay, but too much fire makes the warrior callous and inhumane, and he himself will get burned as well." "Water" represents the virtue of compassion. "Humans need water to survive, but again, too much water causes flooding and is hazardous." Excessive compassion also brings a mare's nest of epic proportions through a lack of sincerity. Like yin and yang in the universe, equilibrium is paramount.

"The civic and military virtues are like two wings of a bird." Among civic virtues are "compassion and courtesy, or a sense of propriety." Under the wing of martial virtue are the ideals of "duty and courage."

The warrior must be erudite enough to abide by these standards of moral excellence. "To do this with a sincere heart requires absolute faith in one's inherent nature." It is only then, according to Tansai, "that the Samurai can be an authentic guardian of the people."

Loyalty Means Peace of Mind

中 + 心 = HEART IN MIDDLE = CENTERED MIND
= LOYALTY = PEACE OF MIND

Furthermore, it is the duty of a warrior to act only in the name of justice, not out of an egotistical craving for honor or rewards. Strong determination is needed to maintain poise and decorum because a "Samurai's profession is fraught with dangers forcing him to become a vicious beast bereft of any human decency."

To exemplify generosity in behavior and manners, Tansai believed that the warrior must "always seek perfection through rigorous self-reflection." This is how a warrior survives and thrives in his responsibilities to his brotherhood and society.

Loyalty has always been fundamental in the Way of the warrior, but many Samurai, according to Tansai, "are mistaken in their understanding of the concept." He argued that sworn loyalty was not just a matter of throwing oneself wholeheartedly into the service of one's lord, or making the ultimate sacrifice fighting to the death. It also was not simply showing conviction of one's ideals in the face of intense adversity. Of course, these are important. True faithfulness was to go about one's business without seeking accolades or profit. "Discard one's vanity in protecting your lord. Never boast of exploits. Just strive for excellence and keep toiling for the greater good."

The ultimate expression of loyalty was to have "peace of mind." In other words, "the Samurai must be satisfied he is earning his stipend through genuine contributions, and not savoring a reputation he does not deserve." Concealing his shortcomings and glossing over his ineffectiveness should, presuming he is of good conscience, leave him feeling extremely uneasy. Deficiencies notwithstanding, the answer to this dilemma, Tansai proposes, is all in the Samurai's attitude. "As long as he is devoted to protecting the world against dishonest or illegal behavior whatever the cost, then he has nothing to feel ashamed of. This is what gives him peace of mind." This is true loyalty.

Daidoji Yuzan (1639–1730)
大道寺友山

7. Die in Your Bed

Military scholar Daidoji Yuzan wrote *Budo Shoshinshu* (1725), a popular self-help book to guide Samurai on the right path. As we have seen, Yuzan's teachers, Yamaga Soko and Hojo Ujinaga, were celebrated scholars and strategists, and his works were a logical extension of their teachings. Incidentally, both men were students of Obata Kagenori, compiler of *Koyo-gunkan*.

Yuzan trained in the classics, such as the *Analects of Confucius* and the philosophy of Mencius, and deliberated on how these philosophies could best be applied to Samurai conduct of his time. He embraced the Confucian-inspired view that Samurai should live as "superior men" in the world. Above all, he proclaimed that "a Samurai should accept that his body and life are not his." To fulfill his weighty burden of service, the Samurai must be ready to do whatever his lord directs him to do. "One must treasure his life, avoid intemperance in eating, drinking, and indulging carnal desires. A Samurai must endeavor to live even one day longer so that he can serve his lord to the very end."

Daidoji Yuzan's Teachers

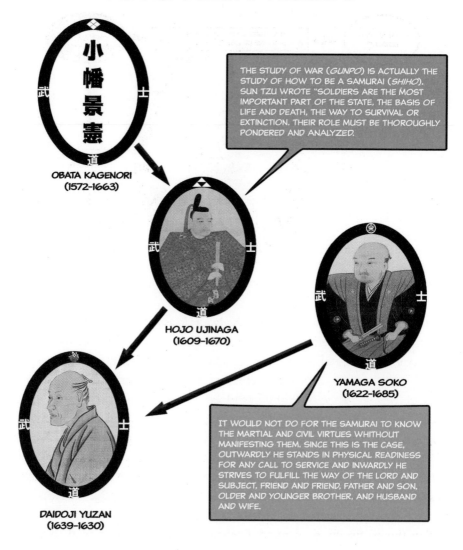

小幡景憲

OBATA KAGENORI
(1572-1663)

THE STUDY OF WAR (*GUNPO*) IS ACTUALLY THE STUDY OF HOW TO BE A SAMURAI (*SHIHO*). SUN TZU WROTE "SOLDIERS ARE THE MOST IMPORTANT PART OF THE STATE, THE BASIS OF LIFE AND DEATH, THE WAY TO SURVIVAL OR EXTINCTION. THEIR ROLE MUST BE THOROUGHLY PONDERED AND ANALYZED.

HOJO UJINAGA
(1609-1670)

YAMAGA SOKO
(1622-1685)

DAIDOJI YUZAN
(1639-1630)

IT WOULD NOT DO FOR THE SAMURAI TO KNOW THE MARTIAL AND CIVIL VIRTUES WHITHOUT MANIFESTING THEM. SINCE THIS IS THE CASE, OUTWARDLY HE STANDS IN PHYSICAL READINESS FOR ANY CALL TO SERVICE AND INWARDLY HE STRIVES TO FULFILL THE WAY OF THE LORD AND SUBJECT, FRIEND AND FRIEND, FATHER AND SON, OLDER AND YOUNGER BROTHER, AND HUSBAND AND WIFE.

Counter to the usual expectation, Yuzan preaches that dying from old age in bed is a fitting end for a Samurai. Engaging in meaningless disagreements resulting in the bloody deaths of friends or risking injury to oneself is, he points out, the height of disloyalty and to be avoided at all costs. "Be he of high rank or low, a man who puts death out of his mind will lead an unhealthy life of overeating, drunkenness, and lechery." Accordingly, he will suffer illnesses of the spleen and kidneys and die prematurely. "Even if he lives, he will subsist as a good-for-nothing burden who is consistently under the weather." He who is ever mindful of death will appear younger than he really is and will always be hale and hearty.

Confucian Peace-time Bushi Ethos

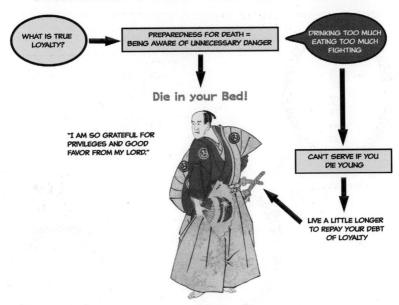

WHAT IS TRUE LOYALTY?

PREPAREDNESS FOR DEATH = BEING AWARE OF UNNECESSARY DANGER

DRINKING TOO MUCH EATING TOO MUCH FIGHTING

Die in your Bed!

"I AM SO GRATEFUL FOR PRIVILEGES AND GOOD FAVOR FROM MY LORD."

CAN'T SERVE IF YOU DIE YOUNG

LIVE A LITTLE LONGER TO REPAY YOUR DEBT OF LOYALTY

Furthermore, Yuzan's reasoning for always keeping death at the forefront of his mind was to foster attributes such as tolerance, modesty, balance, and a realization of the fragility of the human condition. "Mindfulness of one's mortality," he declares, "is required of a Samurai lest he squander his life in frivolity and excess, cutting short the time and usefulness of his tenure in service." The ideal was to "live long and prosper," not to destroy the gift of life in a momentary or perhaps endless lapse of reason.

From its very first pages, *Budo Shoshinshu* emphasizes continuous awareness of death as the Samurai's most important mental mission. The instant a Samurai takes his chopsticks to pluck lumps of rice cake from porridge on New Year's Day until the very last moment on the eve of the next, he must keep death, above all other things, firmly in his mind. Constantly thinking about death, a Samurai simultaneously treads the path of loyalty to his lord and filial piety to his parents.

No matter what ill-fortune or calamity befalls him, he will triumph and live a long and useful life with this attitude. What's more, he will become a better person for it. Yuzan goes on to note that failure to contemplate death will invite "unforeseen catastrophe and cause the Samurai inadvertently to sully the name of his lord." Living even one day longer was the finest way to demonstrate his devotion and gratitude. It was also a candid warning about how quickly things could spiral out of control when unpredictable, inebriated Samurai from rival clans roamed the streets of Edo with blood-lusting swords at their sides. It was a recipe for disaster to not take great care at all times.

Judgment Day

FOR THE MAN WHO WOULD BE A WARRIOR, REGARDLESS OF HIGH OR LOW RANK, HIS VERY FIRST CONSIDERATION SHOULD BE THE QUALITY OF THE MOMENT OF HIS PHYSICAL END, WHEN HIS TIME RUNS OUT

GOODBYE MY FRIENDS. IT'S BEEN AN HONOR

I, TANAKA SHINUNOSUKE, HAVE NO REGRETS AND AM PROUD TO DIE FOR MY LORD.

Budo Shoshinshu also emphasizes the importance of family life and cordial relationships with everyone in one's orbit, and gives the usual advice about studying the classics and maintaining military skills. Heaven forbid any Samurai so cowardly and contemptible who would raise a hand to his wife!

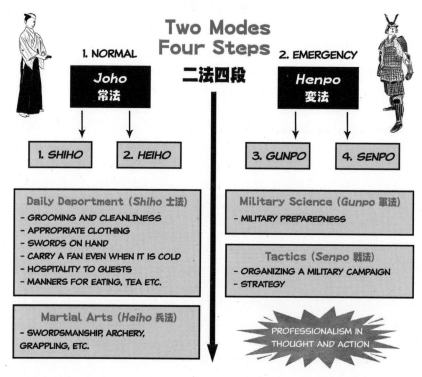

Two Modes Four Steps
二法四段

1. NORMAL

Joho 常法

2. EMERGENCY

Henpo 変法

1. SHIHO

2. HEIHO

3. GUNPO

4. SENPO

Daily Deportment (Shiho 士法)
- GROOMING AND CLEANLINESS
- APPROPRIATE CLOTHING
- SWORDS ON HAND
- CARRY A FAN EVEN WHEN IT IS COLD
- HOSPITALITY TO GUESTS
- MANNERS FOR EATING, TEA ETC.

Military Science (Gunpo 軍法)
- MILITARY PREPAREDNESS

Tactics (Senpo 戦法)
- ORGANIZING A MILITARY CAMPAIGN
- STRATEGY

Martial Arts (Heiho 兵法)
- SWORDSMANSHIP, ARCHERY, GRAPPLING, ETC.

PROFESSIONALISM IN THOUGHT AND ACTION

Yuzan reaffirms the warriors' identity and prescribes a concise code of conduct for daily life with his "Two Modes and Four Steps." Every subcategory required nothing less that full attention and provided a means to exhibit outstanding character. This was a way of accumulating an admirable reputation instead of demonstrating prowess in battle.

Muro Kyuso (1658–1734)
室鳩巣

8. The Way of Self-Cultivation

Muro Kyuso was a Neo-Confucian scholar who served Maeda Tsunanori of the Kanazawa domain (present-day Ishikawa Prefecture). He is otherwise known as Muro Naokiyo. The cottage he lived in was named "Pigeon Nest" and it is from these ideograms that he adopted the name Kyuso.

Kyuso was sent to study in Kyoto and gained such a fine reputation that prominent scholar-statesman Arai Hakuseki recommended him in 1711 for the coveted post of "Confucian professor" for the shogunate. The 8th shogun, Tokugawa Yoshimune, established a separate school in 1719 and Kyuso was appointed as one of the main teachers.

Counter to the general trend, he was opposed to the "Japanization" of Neo-Confucianism, preferring instead a more traditional approach in line with orthodox Chinese teachings. He wrote several influential books, including *Ako Gijin-roku* (1703) in which he defended the actions of the famous 47-Ronin, and *Sundai Zatsuwa* (1732), which contains a collection of his lectures. The following "Ten Rules for Warriors" is found in his book *Meikun Kakun* (Family Precepts of the Enlightened Ruler, 1715).

Kyuso's theories for self-cultivation were based on the concept of *shindoku* ("vigilance in solitude"). This means that the warrior should not in any way try to conceal mistakes but be confident that if his mind was pure and he did not forget the "three debts" of gratitude to parents, lord, and the sages, any error on his part could be pardoned.

Muro Kyuso's Warrior Ideal

DO NOT LIE

DO NOT BE SELFISH

ACT WITH CORRECT DEPORTMENT

NEVER CURRY FAVOR WITH THOSE ABOVE OR PICK ON THOSE BELOW

DO NOT BAD MOUTH OTHERS

NEVER BREAK A PROMISE

DO NOT FORSAKE THE PREDICAMENT OF THE PEOPLE

DO NOT DO WHAT MUST NOT BE DONE

NEVER STEP BACK WHEN IT IS TIME TO DIE

VALUE RIGHT REASON

Kyuso taught that benevolence is a man's original vital force (*ki*). *Ki* of the body is one's pulse and *ki* of the heart is love. "If the pulse stops, the body will die. In the same way, if love dies, the heart will stop." Benevolence, he argues, is precisely the "life force of the heart." He underscores *gi* (right reason) as an essential arrow in the Samurai's quiver, but believed a superior warrior was not overly complicated. "He simply needs to act selflessly, with honesty and integrity."

Yamamoto Jocho (1659–1719)
山本常朝

9. To Die, or Not to Die

Yamamoto Jocho (aka Tsunetomo) served the Nabeshima lords in the Saga do-main. When Nabeshima Mitsushige died in 1700, it was Jocho's declared inten-tion to follow him to the netherworld. This was the greatest expression of devotion a warrior could show in peacetime. Ritual suicide by disembowelment (*seppuku*), known as *junshi* or *oibara*, had been outlawed in the Saga domain in 1661 and by a national decree issued by the shogunate in 1663 as too many warriors were killing themselves on the passing of their lords through personal choice, or from peer pressure, as their grand farewell to the mundane world and final display of bravery and trustworthiness.

Denied this honor, Jocho chose to hang up his swords and take the tonsure, leaving clan service to live out his remaining years meditatively in a thatched hut. *Hagakure* is a memoir of lamentations by a loyal retainer thwarted in his stubborn desire to perform a suicidal swansong of fidelity.

Tashiro Tsuramoto's Career

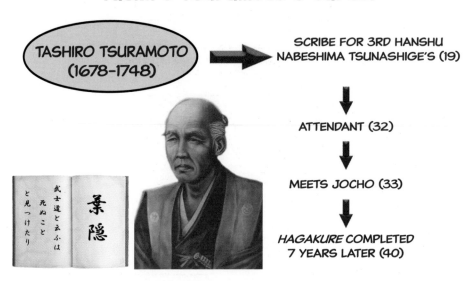

TASHIRO TSURAMOTO
(1678–1748)

SCRIBE FOR 3RD HANSHU
NABESHIMA TSUNASHIGE'S (19)

ATTENDANT (32)

MEETS JOCHO (33)

HAGAKURE COMPLETED
7 YEARS LATER (40)

Hagakure was written in the early 18th century. A self-professed catastrophist, Yamamoto Jocho spoke of his pessimistic view of the world and his reminiscences of historical events to his junior colleague, Tashiro Tsuramoto. Tsuramoto visited Jocho over the course of seven years at his little hermitage in the mountains of Saga and diligently recorded their discussions for posterity. However, that may not have been the intention, for Jocho instructed Tsuramoto to "burn the text" once completed.

Jocho expresses great regret at how young Samurai "talk of money, about profit and loss, their household financial problems, taste in fashion, and idle chatter of sex." Preoccupation with frivolities and with materialism was symptomatic of new generations of warriors who had never experienced battle and therefore lacked discipline and the purity of intent characteristic of previous generations.

Indisputably the most famous phrase in *Hagakure* is "The Way of the warrior is found in dying." Despite its seeming simplicity, this equivocal challenge is open to interpretation. Did Jocho really mean that warriors should gleefully seize any opportunity to die? "If one is faced with two options of life or death, simply settle for death. It is not an especially difficult choice; just go forth and meet it confidently." This would suggest that it was indeed the case. Conversely, the very next sentence in the text provides a literal and figurative juxtaposition. "Only when you constantly live as though already a corpse (*joju shinimi*) will you be able to find freedom in the martial Way and be able to fulfill your tasks without fault throughout your life."

Hagakure's Message—"Crisis Means Chance"

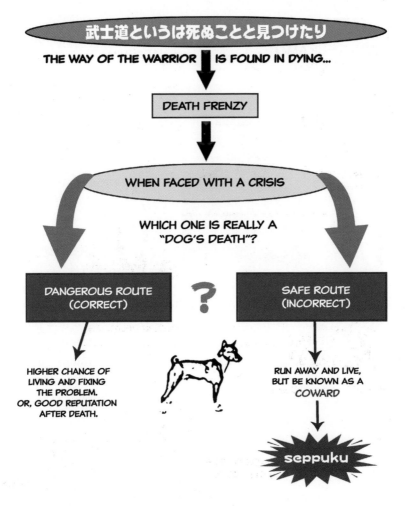

武士道というは死ぬことと見つけたり

THE WAY OF THE WARRIOR IS FOUND IN DYING...

DEATH FRENZY

WHEN FACED WITH A CRISIS

WHICH ONE IS REALLY A "DOG'S DEATH"?

DANGEROUS ROUTE (CORRECT)

SAFE ROUTE (INCORRECT)

HIGHER CHANCE OF LIVING AND FIXING THE PROBLEM. OR, GOOD REPUTATION AFTER DEATH.

RUN AWAY AND LIVE, BUT BE KNOWN AS A COWARD

seppuku

The literal meaning of the proclamation "death over life" is to "live as if dead," remembering that every second of life is a precious, inimitable moment not to be squandered. If you think of yourself as already dead, what is there to be afraid of? What is the worst thing that can happen? No task in the world is too hard for a man who has no fear of his mortality.

A lower ranked Samurai was obliged to serve as if in a "frenzy of death with purity of intent." In reality, he had no direct influence on how the domain was governed and no right to counsel his lord in person. His only way of contributing to the domain and paying homage to his lord was to figuratively sacrifice his flesh in "virtual service." Although mostly invisible to his lord, his single-minded zeal in performing his duties and any thankless task as if he had nothing to lose is what gave meaning to his existence.

Different Ranks Different Expectations

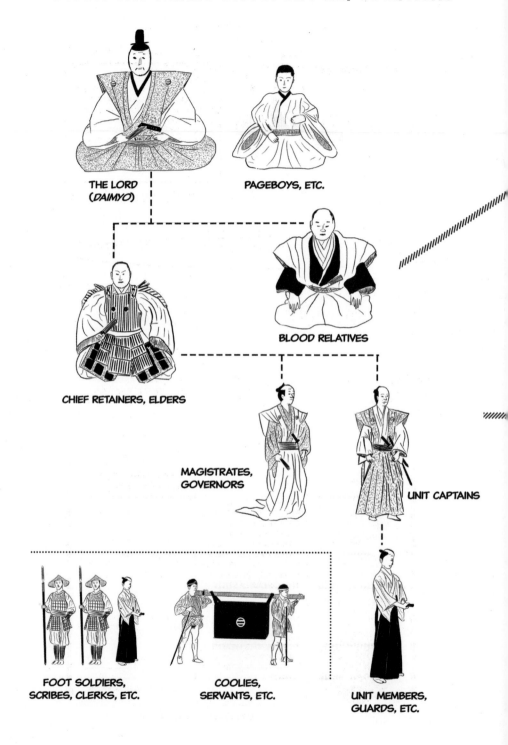

THE LORD
(*DAIMYO*)

PAGEBOYS, ETC.

BLOOD RELATIVES

CHIEF RETAINERS, ELDERS

MAGISTRATES,
GOVERNORS

UNIT CAPTAINS

FOOT SOLDIERS,
SCRIBES, CLERKS, ETC.

COOLIES,
SERVANTS, ETC.

UNIT MEMBERS,
GUARDS, ETC.

LOYALTY of COUNSEL
(Higher Warriors)

UPPER-LEVEL SAMURAI

GREAT LOYALTY

HONOR FOUND IN *GOOD COUNSEL* AND *REMONSTRANCE* THROUGH SELFLESS ADVICE FOR THE GOOD OF THE LORD AND DOMAIN, WISDOM AND DISCRETION, PREPAREDNESS TO PROTECT OR DIE TO TAKE RESPONSIBILITY EVEN IF THE LORD IS A FOOL.

PURE WILL (*ICHINEN*)

> "The Way of the Warrior is found in dying"

"DEATH FRENZY"
死に狂い (*Shinigurui*)
(Lower-ranked Warriors)

Ichinen

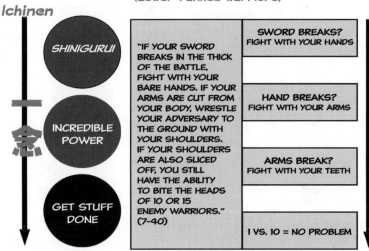

SHINIGURUI

INCREDIBLE POWER

GET STUFF DONE

"IF YOUR SWORD BREAKS IN THE THICK OF THE BATTLE, FIGHT WITH YOUR BARE HANDS. IF YOUR ARMS ARE CUT FROM YOUR BODY, WRESTLE YOUR ADVERSARY TO THE GROUND WITH YOUR SHOULDERS. IF YOUR SHOULDERS ARE ALSO SLICED OFF, YOU STILL HAVE THE ABILITY TO BITE THE HEADS OF 10 OR 15 ENEMY WARRIORS." (7-40)

SWORD BREAKS?
FIGHT WITH YOUR HANDS

HAND BREAKS?
FIGHT WITH YOUR ARMS

ARMS BREAK?
FIGHT WITH YOUR TEETH

1 VS. 10 = NO PROBLEM

LIVE AS IF ALREADY DEAD...

What is a *Kusemono*?

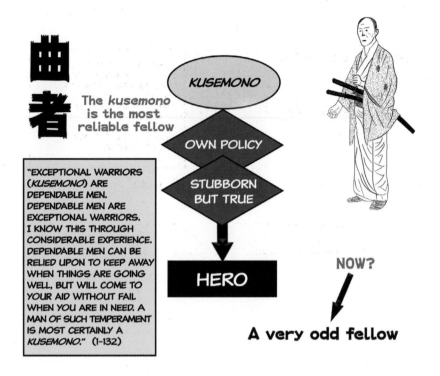

曲者

The *kusemono*
is the most
reliable fellow

"EXCEPTIONAL WARRIORS
(*KUSEMONO*) ARE
DEPENDABLE MEN.
DEPENDABLE MEN ARE
EXCEPTIONAL WARRIORS.
I KNOW THIS THROUGH
CONSIDERABLE EXPERIENCE.
DEPENDABLE MEN CAN BE
RELIED UPON TO KEEP AWAY
WHEN THINGS ARE GOING
WELL, BUT WILL COME TO
YOUR AID WITHOUT FAIL
WHEN YOU ARE IN NEED. A
MAN OF SUCH TEMPERAMENT
IS MOST CERTAINLY A
KUSEMONO." (1-132)

KUSEMONO

OWN POLICY

STUBBORN
BUT TRUE

HERO

NOW?

A very odd fellow

On the other hand, the "loyalty of counsel" was reserved for upper ranking Samurai. To fulfill their important duty of advising their lord and cautioning him about his immoral or unfair behavior required considerable diplomacy and discretion. Honor was found in the act of carefully offering advice. Angering the lord came with a real risk of death although such an act of self-sacrifice was precisely what constituted the warrior's Way.

In both virtual and counsel-based loyalty, the necessary mindset was unwavering will and intent, referred to throughout the pages of *Hagakure* as *ichinen*. A warrior who could exhibit such resolve and purity in thought and action was hailed as a *kusemono*. In modern Japanese language, *kusemono* negatively connotes an eccentric or abnormal person. The *kusemono* in *Hagakure*, however, represents a dependable warrior. Such a man could be always be relied on to appear in the midst of a calamity and toil behind the scenes when not needed. He was, for all intents and purposes, a superhero.

The spirit of *Hagakure* and the heroic *kusemono* can best be summed up by the simple clan oath set out at the very start of the book: "Never lag behind others in the pursuit of the Way of the warrior. Be ready to serve one's lord. Honour one's parents. Serve for the benefit of others with a heart of great compassion."

The Quality of Victory

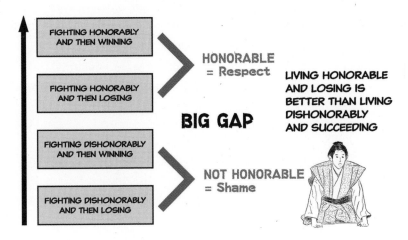

Contests between Samurai ended in one of four results: a graceful victory, a disgraceful victory, a graceful defeat, or a disgraceful defeat. The underlying premise in this aesthetic of competition is, "how you win and how you lose are equivalent to how you live and how you die." In the world of the Samurai, a graceful, honorable defeat was considered far superior to a disgraceful, deceitful victory, even though losing meant death in mortal combat. And, life was the greatest battle of all.

Izawa Nagahide (1668–1730)
井沢長秀

10. A Shinto Outlook

Izawa Nagahide was a Shinto scholar who trained under Yamazaki Ansai (1619–82), founder of Suika Shinto. He served the Hosokawa clan in Kyushu (Higo Kumamoto domain). An expert in the martial arts of *jujutsu* and *kenjutsu*, Naga-hide wrote numerous essays on warrior ideals centered on his studies in national learning (*kokugaku*) and the Chinese classics. He also wrote a war tale, *Kikuchi Sasagunki*, and a book of life precepts called *Bushi-kun* (1715). The latter consists of five volumes, but owing to its popularity was revised and expanded to ten volumes in 1720.

Although Nagahide followed the usual line of giving one's all to foster a balance between *bun* and *bu* (martial and cultural affairs), he was not afraid to criticize the status quo. He was critical of such popular notions as studying Zen as the quickest way to become efficient in sword work, and pinning one's hopes on learning combat skills by observing those of mythical creatures such as *tengu*. He maintained these notions were nonsensical and were concocted by charlatans teaching dubious techniques and philosophies for profit.

Being a scholar of Shinto and Japanese history, Nagahide's works included various religious influences and analogies to describe typical warrior models. Stating that Samurai culture is as old as Japan itself, he explains how the Way of the warrior is inextricably linked with the divine origins of Japan.

Jewel = Flexibility

Mirror = Rectitude

Sword = Resoluteness

Comparing the qualities of the warrior with the "Three Imperial Regalia" (jewel, mirror, and sword) he argued that the jewel, with its subtle curved shape, represents flexibility and the spirit of humanity and bene-volence with which the world should be governed. The mirror epitomizes uprightness and integrity. Whatever is reflected in the shiny surface of the mirror is never distorted but is revealed in its true form, warts and all. "Nothing can be concealed, and so the heart of the warrior must be genuinely clear and pure."

Honesty prevails over corruption. The sword denotes a mind not intimidated by difficulty, danger, or disappointment, one that is decisive and capable of casting aside covetous people within and chastises evil for the blessing of all.

"A warrior who has mastered the martial and civil arts must conceal his strengths and courage rather than ooze a threatening, arrogant presence." Naga-hide points out that "temperate men" were by and large weak whereas "strong men" tended to be abrasive and uncouth. To rectify these flaws, Nagahide recommended that the Samurai "should first be taught to read and write to become conversant with the refined things in life and to digest moral standards to guide one's carriage." Only then was it safe for the Samurai to study martial arts. He insisted that a "balance of firmness and acquiescence was indispensable for averting bawdiness or impotence." Wearing a scowl of violent intent was symptomatic of a Samurai deviating from his true path. "In such a spiritual state, he cannot serve as a loyal, dutiful retainer."

Izawa Nagahide's Warrior Ideal

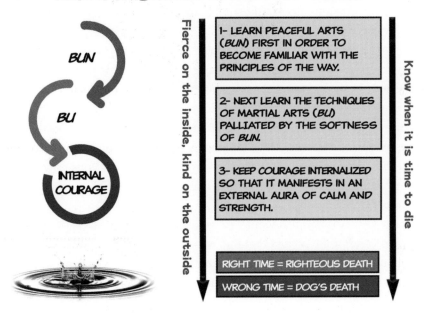

BUN

BU

INTERNAL COURAGE

Fierce on the inside, kind on the outside

Know when it is time to die

1– LEARN PEACEFUL ARTS (*BUN*) FIRST IN ORDER TO BECOME FAMILIAR WITH THE PRINCIPLES OF THE WAY.

2– NEXT LEARN THE TECHNIQUES OF MARTIAL ARTS (*BU*) PALLIATED BY THE SOFTNESS OF *BUN*.

3– KEEP COURAGE INTERNALIZED SO THAT IT MANIFESTS IN AN EXTERNAL AURA OF CALM AND STRENGTH.

RIGHT TIME = RIGHTEOUS DEATH

WRONG TIME = DOG'S DEATH

Being brave on the inside but kind-hearted on the outside was a major quality. Nonetheless, as a professional man-at-arms, "the Samurai must always be prepared to forfeit his life in action and be ready to go into the breach without a second thought." That is not to say that life was to be sacrificed lightly. The trick was to know when to die. "The ability to know this moment is commendable, whereas dying at the wrong time is a 'dog's death.'"

When the Samurai enters the fray, his technique should "envelop the enemy like a rock in water, not clash like rock on rock." This was to use one's energy to smother the enemy and is precisely the principle that judo is based on: flexibility overcoming hardness.

Hakuin Ekaku (1686–1769)
白隠慧鶴

11. A Zen Outlook

Hakuin Ekaku was the son of a Samurai but he joined the priesthood at fifteen and made a name for himself as a writer and artist. Hakuin was instrumental in popularizing the Rinzai sect of Zen and chose to live frugally among the parishioners of the Shoin-ji Temple at the foot of Mount Fuji. Hakuin instructed his disciples in the principles of Zen by means of question and answer using *koan* riddles to achieve spiritual insight. He formulated arguably the most famous *koan* of all: "Two hands clap and there is a sound. What is the sound of one hand?"

Hakuin was also a renowned calligrapher. His brush strokes are powerful and are extolled by experts as being indicative of an enlightened mind. Of his many manuscripts, *Oradegama* (1749) contains a sermon to Lord Nabeshima (1702–49) of Settsu Province about the importance of training the body and mind for health's sake, which ultimately extends to the well-being of the land and its people. In another essay, *Oniazami* (1751), he recommends that Samurai commit body and soul to service and cultivate courage through contemplating death and the meaning of his "one-hand" *koan*.

Hakuin writes that "essence, energy, and spirit" are the main ingredients of the human form. As such, "a cultivated individual takes good care of their energy and does not squander it." He compares the "art of nourishing life" with the wisdom required for governance: the leader (*daimyo*) is its "spirit"; officials or ministers (Samurai retainers) are its "essence"; and people provide the "energy" of the realm. When the people are shown love and compassion, the country will prosper just as the human body will be fortified through meditation. When the country's people create pandemonium, the country itself will disintegrate, just as the human body perishes when its energy is spent. For this reason, Hakuin contends that "the wise leader always affords due attention to the common people, while the ignoramus permits his officers to have their way and engage in selfish, exploitative activities."

Hakuin Ekaku's Warrior Ideal

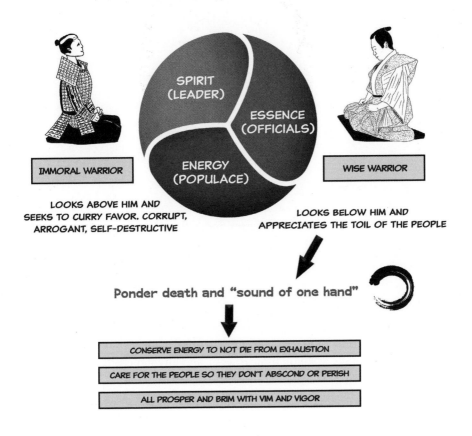

SPIRIT (LEADER)

ESSENCE (OFFICIALS)

ENERGY (POPULACE)

IMMORAL WARRIOR

WISE WARRIOR

LOOKS ABOVE HIM AND SEEKS TO CURRY FAVOR. CORRUPT, ARROGANT, SELF-DESTRUCTIVE

LOOKS BELOW HIM AND APPRECIATES THE TOIL OF THE PEOPLE

Ponder death and "sound of one hand"

CONSERVE ENERGY TO NOT DIE FROM EXHAUSTION

CARE FOR THE PEOPLE SO THEY DON'T ABSCOND OR PERISH

ALL PROSPER AND BRIM WITH VIM AND VIGOR

Yoshida Shoin (1830–59)
吉田松陰

12. Modern Martyr

Yoshida Shoin (Norikata) was born in the village of Matsumoto near the Mori clan's castle town of Choshu (present-day Yamaguchi Prefecture). A gifted author and charismatic teacher, Shoin was also highly proficient in the military arts. He is perhaps best known as a key activist for the anti-foreign *sonno-joi* movement (Revere the Emperor, Expel the Barbarians), whose teachings were largely influenced by Yamaga Soko's doctrine.

In 1854, Shoin attempted to stow away on Commodore Matthew Perry's "Black Ship," the USS *Powhatan*, to learn more about what Japan was up against. Ironically, this was in breach of the *National Seclusion Law*, which forbade Japanese people from leaving the country, and he was placed under arrest in 1855.

Shoin opened a private school called the Shoka Sonjuku where he politically inspired several young Samurai who would later play a prominent role in the Meiji Restoration of 1868. His ideology led him to plot the assassination of an official in the shogunate. The attempt was unsuccessful and he was imprisoned again and executed for sedition at the age of twenty-nine.

Shoin's literary works include *Kaikoroku* (Record of the Past, 1855), *Kokokushi* (Aspirations of a Hero, 1858), and *Ryukonroku* (Record of an Everlasting Spirit, 1858). The following synopsis of his warrior ideals was written on a scroll as the "Seven Rules for Warriors."

"Seven Rules" for Warriors

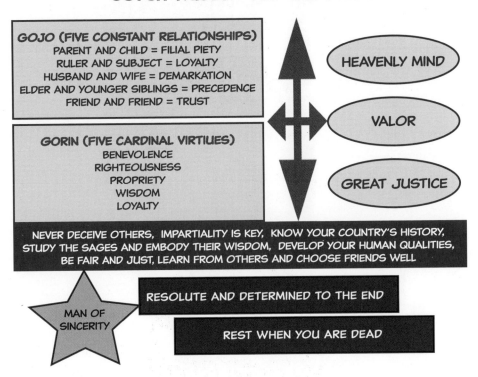

GOJO (FIVE CONSTANT RELATIONSHIPS)
PARENT AND CHILD = FILIAL PIETY
RULER AND SUBJECT = LOYALTY
HUSBAND AND WIFE = DEMARCATION
ELDER AND YOUNGER SIBLINGS = PRECEDENCE
FRIEND AND FRIEND = TRUST

GORIN (FIVE CARDINAL VIRTUES)
BENEVOLENCE
RIGHTEOUSNESS
PROPRIETY
WISDOM
LOYALTY

HEAVENLY MIND

VALOR

GREAT JUSTICE

NEVER DECEIVE OTHERS, IMPARTIALITY IS KEY, KNOW YOUR COUNTRY'S HISTORY, STUDY THE SAGES AND EMBODY THEIR WISDOM, DEVELOP YOUR HUMAN QUALITIES, BE FAIR AND JUST, LEARN FROM OTHERS AND CHOOSE FRIENDS WELL

MAN OF SINCERITY

RESOLUTE AND DETERMINED TO THE END

REST WHEN YOU ARE DEAD

Shoin preached that Samurai must understand the difference between human beings, birds, and animals. The Samurai abided by the "Five Constant Relationships" and the "Five Cardinal Virtues." The "Five Constant Relationships" constituted affection between parent and child, loyalty between ruler and subject demarcation between husband and wife, precedence between elder and younger siblings, and trust between friend and friend. The "Five Cardinal Virtues" were the standard combination of benevolence, righteousness, propriety, wisdom, and loyalty. Of the above, Shoin concluded that "the crucial constituent for humans was loyalty and filial piety."

"We Japanese," he ventured to say, "should know the reason why our country is to be respected in the world. Our imperial family extends back to the beginning of time; our people lay claim to a proud, eternal link to the emperor.... It is incumbent on the warrior to know the history of his land, observe the ancient wisdom of the sages, absorb knowledge from the classics, and make the teachers of antiquity his friends."

The emperor nurtures the people and looks after the business of Japanese ancestors, while the people continue to fulfill the will of their parents by showing reverence to the emperor. "This is what represents the spirit of Japan."

He advocates that nothing was more salient in the Way of the warrior than *gi* (rectitude). *Gi* is kept alive with the spirit of *yu* (valor), and *yu* is validated in safeguarding *gi*. "The Samurai is to be forthright and honest. Duplicity and deceit is the sort of opprobrious conduct for which an warrior should be ashamed." Shoin's life was short but eventful, and even today he is revered in Japan as a man true to his ideals.

Aizu Bushido
会津藩の武士道

13. The Right Path

Samurai from Aizu (present-day Fukushima Prefecture) were known for their nerve in battle and their fierce loyalty. During the Boshin War (1868), which pitted imperial loyalists against the shogunate and its allies, the Aizu domain remained a down-the-line supporter of the shogun.

The Battle of Aizu was one of the fiercest of the war. A few hundred teenage youths in the Byakkotai (White Tiger Brigade), one of four youth reserve units in Aizu, were mobilized against the imperial forces. They were decimated in the Battle of Tonokuchihara on October 8, 1868. A handful of survivors hiked through the forests, over hills, and through an underground stream flowing beneath a mountain to regroup near the Aizu domain's stronghold of Wakamatsu Castle. Emerging from the cool depths of the mountain, they clambered up Iimoriyama hill to get a clearer view of their castle town but were dismayed to see it consumed in smoke. Wrongly assuming their castle had fallen, they climbed further up the hill and all twenty of them, without the slightest hesitation, plunged their short swords deep into their bellies as a last act of defiance and demonstration of self-sacrifice and honor.

The warriors of Aizu personified the ideal of being prepared to renounce one's life in the line of duty. ManyAizu survivors of this tempestuous time later became stalwarts of the Meiji government which they fought to prevent, and diligent officials of modern Japan.

The Consummate Aizu Warrior

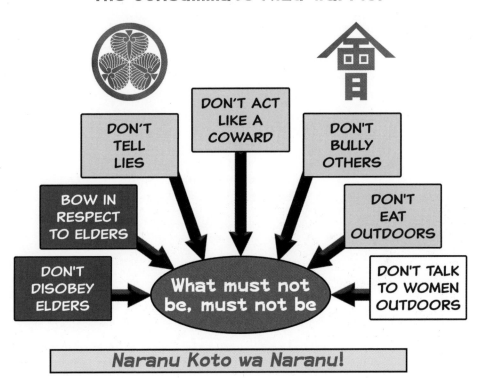

DON'T TELL LIES

DON'T ACT LIKE A COWARD

DON'T BULLY OTHERS

BOW IN RESPECT TO ELDERS

DON'T EAT OUTDOORS

DON'T DISOBEY ELDERS

What must not be, must not be

DON'T TALK TO WOMEN OUTDOORS

Naranu Koto wa Naranu!

The portrait opposite is of Matsudaira Katanobu, *daimyo* of the Aizu domain, who created the famous Nisshinkan school to educate young Samurai in his charge. Byakkotai members were all students at the school.

Aizu is famous for its forthright code of honor. Most of the pronouncements would not be out of place at any time or in any culture. The last one, "Do not talk to women outdoors" is sure to raise a few eyebrows but was not meant in the misogynistic sense that offends modern sensibilities. Aizu warriors were sticklers for decorum, and cavorting with the opposite sex in public was seen as inappropriate behavior for a gentleman warrior and as demeaning to women. A crucial aspect of Aizu Bushido was the role that women played in educating their sons and supporting their husbands in their duties.

So stoic were the womenfolk of Aizu, they also stood out as fearless combatants in the defense of their town during the Boshin War. Many took their own lives in ritual suicide to avoid the indignity of defeat at the hands of the enemy. There are first-hand accounts of enemy warriors brought to tears at what they witnessed.

More than anything, the Aizu Samurai ethos is represented by the simple but profound maxim *Naranu koto wa naranu* ("What must not be, must not be"). In other words, "one must always do what is right." This is the embodiment of Aizu bushido and is the adhesive that binds it together. It is the Samurai's responsibility to act in a way befitting one's station, to show compassion to others, and be steadfast in one's convictions.

To waver in any way, come what may, "must not be." The young Samurai in Aizu's Nisshinkan were strictly schooled to be typical partisans of the Way of the warrior in addition to academic subjects. This was the fundamental principle that all Aizu Samurai learned and embodied from the moment they could stand on their own two feet.

Graves of the Byakko-tai youth who, thinking that the battle had been lost, committed seppuku as their last act of valor. (Photo by the author)

Chapter 5

Nitobe Inazo's Bushido

徳新渡戸稲造の武士道

Nitobe Inazo was born on September 1, 1862, into a Samurai family of the Morioka (aka Nanbu) domain located around modern-day Iwate and Aomori prefectures. Class distinctions were dismantled after the Meiji Restoration, so Nitobe's tenure as a Samurai was not even a decade long. Nevertheless, traditional warrior customs instilled in him during childhood molded his moral outlook. His illustrious career as an educator, civil servant, and diplomat (he served in Geneva as the immensely popular Under-Secretary-General of the League of Nations) can surely be at least partially accredited to his Samurai upbringing.

After studying English in Tokyo, he entered the prestigious government-run Sapporo Agricultural College. It was there that Nitobe converted to Christianity. Hoping to become a "bridge across the Pacific," he enrolled at Tokyo Imperial University to major in economics and literature. Determined to see the world, he cut his studies short and headed to the United States and later Germany for graduate studies. Whilst in the United States, he became a pious Quaker and met his future wife from a prominent Philadelphian Quaker family, Mary Elkinton.

Returning to Japan after six years studying abroad, Nitobe took up a professorial position at his alma mater in Hokkaido. A known workaholic, he resigned through poor health in 1897 and returned to America with Mary to recuperate. It was there that he wrote the most famous of his many books in English, *Bushido:*

The Soul of Japan (1899), first published by a small Quaker publishing house in Philadelphia called Leeds and Biddle. He authored the book with the intention of explaining to Westerners that, even though Japan was not a Christian country, it still had extremely high moral standards of conduct and these derived from the extraordinarily conscientious Samurai.

This little volume was destined to become a leading guide into the mind of the Japanese. After Japan's unexpected triumph in the Russo-Japanese War (1904–5), *Bushido* was translated into many languages. US President Theodore Roosevelt is even reputed to have purchased several dozen copies to distribute to friends and family members. Nitobe's book made "Bushido" internationally recognizable, admired around the world as a code of ethics worthy of emulation.

So popular did Nitobe's book become, detractors such as Tokyo Imperial University philosophy and ethics professor Tetsujiro Inoue (1855–1944), a prolific writer on Bushido in Japan, accused Nitobe of "Christianizing" Samurai thought. Other critics pointed out that Nitobe's Bushido depicted a British public school ethos in Samurai clothing as it cites more Western literature than authentic Samurai sources. Basil Hall Chamberlain (1850–1935), a well-known scholar of things Japanese, denied that Bushido ever existed as a concept and accused Nitobe of "inventing a new religion."

Despite these criticisms, Nitobe's book became the definitive guide on the subject in the West, and following its translation from English to Japanese in 1908 it was treated as a significant addition to the burgeoning genre in Japan. "Bushido" was one of the key words being touted by nationalists as representing the root of "Japanese identity" in the modern era. Nitobe was certainly a patriot, but not a nationalist. He was very much a pacifist and arguably the most internationally minded man of his generation.

Being of Samurai parentage, Nitobe was more qualified than most to publish such an exposition on warrior thought. The criticism of his interpretation of Bushido as being "invented tradition" is undeniable, but all tradition is invented at some time. Each of the strains of Bushido introduced in this book were pertinent to a specific time, region, and people, and to political and social circumstances. What makes these versions more authentic than Inazo's post-Samurai era rendition of Bushido?

Nitobe begins with an explanation of the origins of Bushido and how it was influenced by the religions of Shinto, Buddhism, and Confucianism. Nitobe explains the seven virtues inherent in the warrior's code: rectitude, courage, benevolence, politeness, veracity, honor, and loyalty. He talks of how the Samurai eschewed matters of commerce, were prepared to die to preserve honor, and would never go back on their word.

He also validated the role of the Samurai customs of revenge and *seppuku* (ritual suicide), the role of women in Samurai society, and how, although once exclusively the code of the warrior class, it was through popular culture such as theater and literature that their lofty ideals permeated the hearts of the Japanese. This was made possible by the esteem in which the Samurai, upholders of *noblesse oblige*, were held by the common people.

Nitobe's Bushido represents an inspiring expansion of various traditional virtues remolded to guide modern sensitivities amidst times of monumental change. It remains a bestseller, and any discussion of Bushido in Japan now invariably draws on Nitobe's work as its foundation. This is why I have dedicated the last chapter of this book to it.

1. Making Westerners Understand

Noblesse Oblige

HOW CAN WESTERNERS UNDERSTAND BUSHIDO?

BORROWS EUROPEAN CONCEPT OF NOBLESSE OBLIGE TO EXPLAIN THE WORKINGS OF BUSHIDO

ARISTOCRATS (NOBLES) HAVE AN OBLIGATION TO CARE FOR THOSE NOT AS PRIVILEGED AS THEM

SAMURAI WERE THE PRIVILEGED CLASS IN JAPAN, THEY WERE NOT SUPPOSED TO ABUSE THEIR POWER...

SAMURAI EMBODIED THE VIRTUE OF *JIN* (COMPASSION)

"Chivalry is a flower no less indigenous to the soil of Japan than its emblem, the cherry blossom," suggests Nitobe. He also declares that Bushido is still alive even though Samurai no longer exist, and that it resonates among Japanese people without any tangible shape or form, but still with a moral flavor that makes Japanese "aware that we are still under its potent spell." Although the social conditions through which Bushido evolved have changed drastically, "the light of chivalry ... still illuminates our moral path, surviving its mother institution."

Bushido = Chivalry?

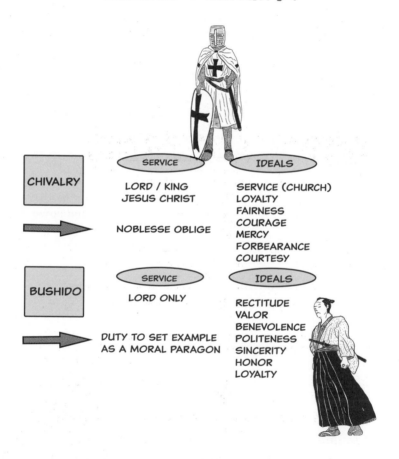

CHIVALRY

SERVICE	IDEALS
LORD / KING JESUS CHRIST	SERVICE (CHURCH) LOYALTY FAIRNESS COURAGE
NOBLESSE OBLIGE	MERCY FORBEARANCE COURTESY

BUSHIDO

SERVICE	IDEALS
LORD ONLY	RECTITUDE VALOR BENEVOLENCE
DUTY TO SET EXAMPLE AS A MORAL PARAGON	POLITENESS SINCERITY HONOR LOYALTY

Nitobe equates the term *noblesse oblige*, as seen in the "Precepts of Knighthood," as a Western ideal that closely resembles the strongly felt principles of the Samurai.

Although Nitobe initially likens "chivalry" to Bushido through various concepts that reveal a crossover in thought, this was merely as an introduction to put the Western reader at ease before delving into the subtle differences that make the Western and Japanese experiences distinct. "The Japanese word which I have roughly rendered chivalry is, in the original, more expressive...."

2. The Ingredients of Bushido

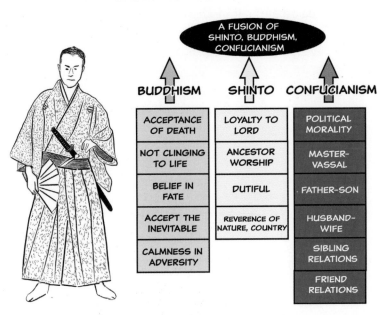

Bushido is ...

A FUSION OF SHINTO, BUDDHISM, CONFUCIANISM

BUDDHISM	SHINTO	CONFUCIANISM
ACCEPTANCE OF DEATH	LOYALTY TO LORD	POLITICAL MORALITY
NOT CLINGING TO LIFE	ANCESTOR WORSHIP	MASTER-VASSAL
BELIEF IN FATE	DUTIFUL	FATHER-SON
ACCEPT THE INEVITABLE	REVERENCE OF NATURE, COUNTRY	HUSBAND-WIFE
CALMNESS IN ADVERSITY		SIBLING RELATIONS
		FRIEND RELATIONS

He further states, "Some words have a national timbre so expressive of race characteristics that the best of translators can do them but scant justice, not to say positive injustice and grievance." He contends that Bushido is not a written code but "consists of a few maxims handed down from mouth to mouth or coming from the pen of some well-known warrior or savant. More frequently it is a code unuttered and unwritten, possessing all the more the powerful sanction of veritable deed, and of a law written on the fleshly tablets of the heart."

Where chivalry draws on the morals of Christianity, the philosophical underpinnings of Bushido according to Nitobe were Buddhism, Shinto, and Confucianism. Each of these religions provided a specific world outlook embraced by the Samurai.

Buddhism "furnished a sense of calm trust in fate, a quiet submission to the inevitable, that stoic composure in sight of danger or calamity, that disdain of life and friendliness with death."

What Buddhism lacked was provided to the Samurai ideal by Shintoism. "Such loyalty to the sovereign, such reverence for ancestral memory, and such filial piety as are not taught by any other creed, were inculcated by the Shinto doctrines, imparting passivity to the otherwise arrogant character of the Samurai. The tenets of Shintoism cover the two predominating features of the emotional life of our race—Patriotism and Loyalty."

Confucian teachings provided the most "prolific source of Bushido"—the "five moral relations between master and servant (the governing and the governed), father and son, husband and wife, older and younger brother, and friend and friend—a confirmation of what the race instinct had recognized before Confucian writings were introduced from China." The "Seven Virtues" that Nitobe explains throughout the book were also derived from the Confucian classics.

The Seven Virtues

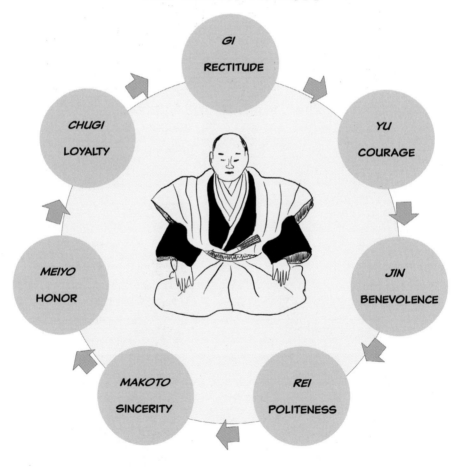

GI
RECTITUDE

YU
COURAGE

CHUGI
LOYALTY

MEIYO
HONOR

JIN
BENEVOLENCE

MAKOTO
SINCERITY

REI
POLITENESS

Rectitude (*Gi* 義) = Supreme Reason

RECTITUDE IS "THE RIGHTEOUS WAY"

MENCIUS (孟子)

"BENEVOLENCE IS A MAN'S MIND, AND RECTITUDE OR RIGHTEOUSNESS IS HIS PATH"

GI (RECTITUDE) = HARD   BOTH VITAL TO SAMURAI
JIN (BENEVOLENCE) = SOFT

GI = ULTIMATE HONORABLE DEPORTMENT

Nitobe starts with the virtue of *gi*, which he calls "rectitude" or "justice." Nothing is more loathsome to a Samurai, Nitobe argues, than "underhand dealings and crooked undertakings." It goes fully against the reasoning of *gi*. "Rectitude is the power of deciding upon a certain course of conduct in accordance with reason, without wavering—to die when it is right to die, to strike when it is right to strike." Furthermore, "Rectitude is the bone that gives firmness and stature. As without bones the head cannot rest on the top of the spine, nor hands move nor feet stand, so without rectitude neither talent nor learning can make of a human frame a Samurai. With it the lack of accomplishments is as nothing."

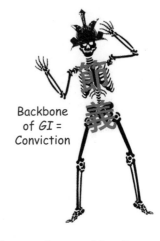

Backbone of *GI* = Conviction

Being daring in battle was hardly considered a virtue among Samurai unless it was demonstrated for some righteous cause. Simply put, "Courage is doing what is right." As is often quoted in Samurai literature through the centuries, "death for a cause unworthy of dying for was called a 'dog's death.'" Charging to certain death in the thick of battle was not particularly heroic. Anybody can do this if they possess a wish to die. True courage, however, is "to live when it is right to live and to die only when it is right to die."

Bushido Bones

VALOR (*YU*)   +   RECTITUDE (*GI*)

YU---THE RIGHT TIME (*GI*) IS NEEDED TO SHOW VALOR
GI---VALOR IS NEEDED TO DO THE RIGHT THING

"RECTITUDE IS THE POWER OF DECIDING UPON A CERTAIN COURSE OF
CONDUCT IN ACCORDANCE WITH REASON WITHOUT WAVERING; TO DIE
WHEN IT IS RIGHT TO DIE; TO STRIKE WHEN IT IS RIGHT TO STRIKE..."

Valor = Composure

DYNAMIC VALOR   **+**   STATIC VALOR

A TRULY COURAGEOUS MAN
IS
CALM AT ALL TIMES

Valor Education

EDUCATED NOT TO FEAR DEATH	

↓

BUILD UP COURAGE

CULTIVATE *YU* (VALOR)

Good   **Bad**

GREAT VALOR (*TAIGI NO YU*)   FOOLHARDY VALOR (*HIPPU NO YU*)

TO DO WHAT IS RIGHT (*GI*) SENSE OF SAMURAI PRIDE AND IDENTITY   VALOR NOT RELATED TO *GI* TYPICAL OF LOWER CLASSES

Nurturing courage and familiarity with the reality of death was an important task in the Samurai's childhood education. "Pilgrimages to all sorts of uncanny places—to execution grounds, to graveyards, to houses reputed of being haunted, were favorite pastimes of the young. In the days when decapitation was public, not only were small boys sent to witness the ghastly scene, but they were made to visit alone the place in the darkness of night and there to leave a mark of their visit on the trunkless head."

This kind of education surely offends our modern sensibilities, but death was always a central consideration in Samurai culture. A Samurai who was afraid of the dark or was repelled by the sight of blood was of no use to anyone.

4. Equilibrium Between Hard and Soft

Counterbalancing the often inflexible virtues of rectitude and valor required benevolence or *jin*. According to Nitobe, "Love, magnanimity, affection for others, sympathy, and pity, were ever recognized to be supreme virtues, the highest of all the attributes of the human soul." The "tender and mother-like" virtue of benevolence was crucial in a militaristic regime where warriors wielded a disproportionate amount of power and possessed the legal right to use violence against common people if their honor was slighted. "If upright Rectitude and stern Justice were peculiarly masculine, Mercy had the gentleness and the persuasiveness of a feminine nature."

Balancing Bravado with Benevolence

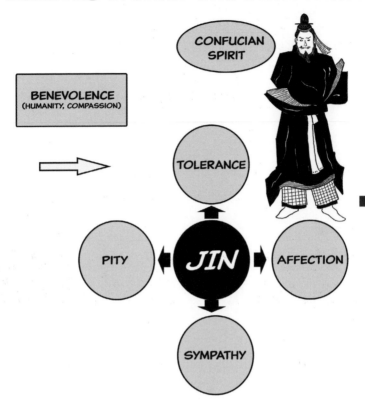

Conversely, Samurai were warned against "indulging in indiscriminate charity, without seasoning it with justice and rectitude." In other words, these virtues acted in tandem as checks and balances for guiding appropriate behavior. As the old maxim went, "The bravest are the tenderest, the loving are the daring." In Japanese, this is read as *Bushi no nasake* or, literally, the "humaneness of a warrior."

Nitobe is careful to point out that mercy or the benevolent spirit of a Samurai was no different to that demonstrated by other people. What made it distinct in the Samurai, however, was that it was "backed with power to save or kill." Furthermore, the Samurai's cultivation of compassion nurtured in his heart "modesty and complaisance, actuated by respect for others' feelings." This was the "root of politeness."

Rei or "politeness" was an integral part of Samurai behavior, as it is in Japan today. Nevertheless, as Nitobe stressed, politeness is worthless if it is feigned only to avoid causing offense. True politeness, he argued, was the "outward manifestation of a sympathetic regard for the feelings of others." Quoting from the Bible in his appraisal of unpretentious politeness, he declares that in its purest form it is akin to "love." "Politeness suffereth long, and is kind; envieth not, vaunteth not itself, is not puffed up; doth not behave itself unseemly, seeketh not her own, is not easily provoked, taketh not account of evil."

Greatest Expression of Politeness

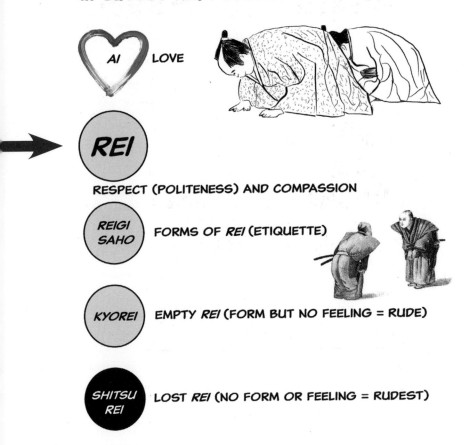

AI — LOVE

REI — RESPECT (POLITENESS) AND COMPASSION

REIGI SAHO — FORMS OF REI (ETIQUETTE)

KYOREI — EMPTY REI (FORM BUT NO FEELING = RUDE)

SHITSU REI — LOST REI (NO FORM OR FEELING = RUDEST)

Referring to the teachings of the time-honored Ogasawara school of Samurai manners, "The end of all etiquette is to so cultivate your mind that even when you are quietly seated, not the roughest ruffian can dare make onset on your person."

Sincere and natural adherence to rules governing politeness and courtesy was almost a religious journey in itself. "By constant exercise in correct manners, one brings all the parts and faculties of his body into perfect order and into such harmony with itself and its environment as to express the mastery of spirit over the flesh."

5. A Samurai's Word

Without "sincerity of intent" politeness becomes but a "farce and a show." A Samurai viewed insincerity, lying, and crookedness as a stain on his honor and

Difference between Samurai and Others

an act of cowardice. His high position in society, Nitobe declares, "demanded a loftier standard of veracity than that of the tradesman and peasant." Thus, sincerity (*makoto*) was a further defining characteristic of the warrior ideal.

Sayings such as *Bushi no ichi-gon* ("A Samurai's word is his bond") indicated that a Samurai's promise was absolute. A true Samurai would never go back on his word; his life was defined by every word he spoke. The thought of putting a guarantee in writing was abhorrent and undignified. "Many thrilling anecdotes were told of those who atoned by death for *ni-gon*, a double tongue."

If words passed a Samurai's lips, then come what may, no matter how big or small, that pledge would be transferred into action. The promise to follow through on any vow could never be compromised.

6. Honor above All

Underpinning all these virtues was an intense preoccupation with honor or, more precisely, the desire to avoid shame. Nitobe describes this as implying a "vivid consciousness of personal dignity and worth." A Samurai's name, his reputation in the demanding community of honor was all he cared about. His honor was "the immortal part of one's self, what remains being bestial...." As such, "any infringement upon its integrity was felt as shame, and the sense of shame (*ren-chi-shin*) was one of the earliest to be cherished in juvenile education." Any slight on a Samurai's honor was like a scar on a tree "which time, instead of effacing, only helps to enlarge."

Interconnecting Virtues

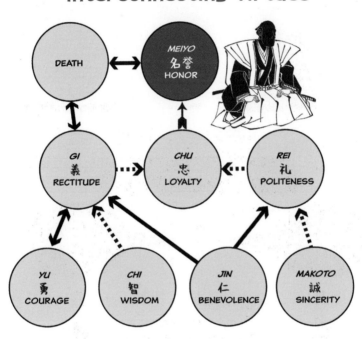

Nitobe describes the intense fear a Samurai held of his name being demeaned as "hanging like Damocles' sword over his head." Although honor was a primary motivation for observing virtuous behavior in his daily life, it also came with considerable peril. Without painstaking attention, the Samurai was prone to overreacting to even the smallest insult. "The morbid excess into which the delicate code of honor was inclined to run was strongly counterbalanced by preaching magnanimity and patience. To take

HONOR
VOLATILE!

PATIENCE
CHILL PILL

offense at slight provocation was ridiculed as 'short-tempered.' The popular adage said: 'To bear what you think you cannot bear is really to bear.'" The preservation of his sense of honor was a precarious balancing act requiring considerable patience and discipline.

7. The Duty of Allegiance

The last of the seven virtues outlined by Nitobe was loyalty—homage and sworn loyalty to a superior. "Of the causes in comparison with which no life was too dear to sacrifice, was the duty of loyalty, which was the keystone making feudal virtues a symmetrical arch."

Loyalty took many different forms and even meant that a Samurai might need to go against the will of his lord. "When a subject differed from his master, the loyal path for him to pursue was to use every available means to persuade him of his error."

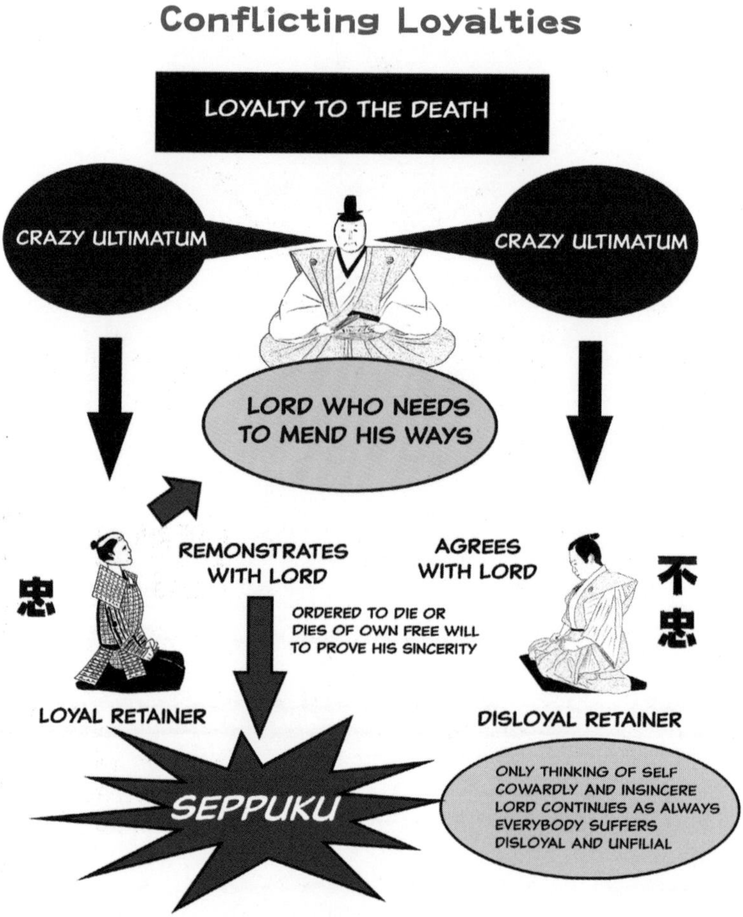

Conflicting Loyalties

LOYALTY TO THE DEATH

CRAZY ULTIMATUM

CRAZY ULTIMATUM

LORD WHO NEEDS TO MEND HIS WAYS

忠

REMONSTRATES WITH LORD

AGREES WITH LORD

不忠

ORDERED TO DIE OR DIES OF OWN FREE WILL TO PROVE HIS SINCERITY

LOYAL RETAINER

DISLOYAL RETAINER

SEPPUKU

ONLY THINKING OF SELF COWARDLY AND INSINCERE LORD CONTINUES AS ALWAYS EVERYBODY SUFFERS DISLOYAL AND UNFILIAL

If a Samurai was unable to persuade his lord of the error of his ways, one course of action that remained was to prove his truthfulness and the depth of his loyalty. He could and often did "make the last appeal to the intelligence and conscience of his lord by demonstrating the sincerity of his words with the shedding of his own blood. Life being regarded as the means whereby to serve his master, and its ideal being set upon honor, the whole education and training of a Samurai were conducted accordingly."

In contrast to the traditional Confucian model in which filial piety to one's parents surpassed loyalty to one's lord, Bushido dictated that the opposite was the correct path. This dichotomy was reconciled by viewing loyalty to the lord as the ultimate expression of filial piety. In other words, it was through his loyal service that the realm and its people could thrive under stable conditions.

The Path to Perfection

CHARACTER
品性

LITERARY ARTS   MILITARY ARTS

SAMURAI CHARACTER IS BORN AND HONED THROUGH HARDSHIP AND TRAINING (SHUGYO)

VALOR
勇

SELF-CONTROL
克己

WISDOM
智

BENEVOLENCE
仁

8. Training Body and Mind

The Samurai's life was one of perpetual study and training. In times of war, he had to be ready to fight. In times of peace, he made sure that he was prepared to execute his duties to the best of his ability. He trained relentlessly in the arts of peace and war, honing his skills, sensitivities, and wisdom as well as consideration for those above and below him.

This demanded immense discipline and self-control. He trained to suffer the insufferable, to embrace his calling with selfless dedication, and to hide any sign of discomfort as it was considered unmanly for him to reveal his emotions. This is how he developed his character.

"The discipline of fortitude on the one hand, inculcating endurance without a groan, and the teaching of politeness on the other, requiring us not to mar the pleasure or serenity of another by expressions of our own sorrow or pain, combined to engender a stoical turn of mind and eventually to confirm it into a national trait of apparent stoicism."

Honor through Hardship

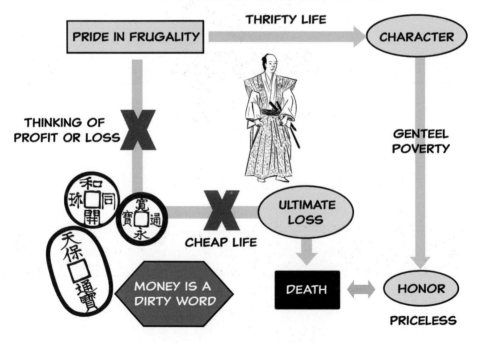

"WHEN HIS STOMACH IS EMPTY,
IT IS A DISGRACE TO FEEL HUNGRY."

Self-control was also evident, for example, in the ideal of genteel poverty. The Samurai abstained from monetary matters of profit and loss. This was the domain of merchants and commoners. It was the Samurai's lot to "bear and face all calamities and adversities with patience and a pure conscience," not to concern himself with the lowly art of making money for personal gain.

Bushido and Yamato-damashii

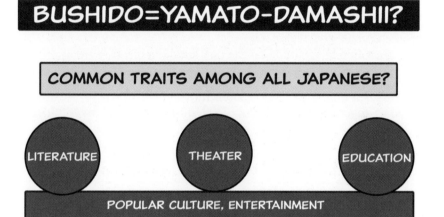

BUSHIDO=YAMATO-DAMASHII?

COMMON TRAITS AMONG ALL JAPANESE?

LITERATURE   THEATER   EDUCATION

POPULAR CULTURE, ENTERTAINMENT

BUSHIDO BECAME POPULAR AMONG THE MASSES → LATER CAME TO REPRESENT THE JAPANESE IDEAL OF HUMANITY = YAMATO-DAMASHII

9. Filtering Down to the Masses

Samurai were a minority in Japanese society. Nitobe claims that their ideals filtered down to the common people and influenced their worldly outlook in profound ways. He suggests that this was made possible through the medium of popular culture.

Today, we still enjoy stories of Samurai heroism in movies and on television. For centuries, the ideals of the Samurai have been the central theme in Kabuki plays, puppet shows, literature, and art, all which were patronized by commoners. "In manifold ways has Bushido filtered down from the social class where it originated, and acted as leaven among the masses, furnishing a moral standard for the whole people. The Precepts of Knighthood, begun at first as the glory of the élite, became in time an aspiration and inspiration to the nation at large; and though the populace could not attain the moral height of those loftier souls, yet Yamato Damashii, the Soul of Japan...."

The last chapter of Nitobe's book predicts the future of Bushido, and is probably more prophetic than the author himself could have imagined. "Bushido as an independent code of ethics may vanish, but its power will not perish from the earth; its schools of martial prowess or civic honor may be demolished, but its light and its glory will long survive their ruins. Like its symbolic flower, after it is blown to the four winds, it will still bless mankind with the perfume with which it will enrich life." The fact that you have this humble explanation of Nitobe's code of ethics in your hand is surely testament to the accuracy of his conclusion.

Front cover of *Bushido: The Soul of Japan*
(Philadelphia Leeds & Biddle, 1900) by Inazo Nitobe.

References

Ansart, O. "Embracing Death: Pure will in *Hagakure.*" *Early Modern Japan: An Interdisciplinary Journal,* Vol. 18 (2010): pp. 57–75.

Asoshina Yasuo (ed.). *Zusetsu, Miyamoto Musashi no Jitsuzō.* Tokyo: Shin Jinbutsu Ōraisha, 2003. Ascii Media Works. *Samurai Graphic Sozai-shu,* 2010.

Bennett, Alexander C. *Bushido and the Art of Living: An Inquiry into Samurai Values.* Tokyo: Japan Library, 2018.

_____. *Hagakure: The Secret Wisdom of the Samurai.* North Clarendon, VT: Tuttle, 2014.

_____. *Japan: The Ultimate Samurai Guide.* North Clarendon, VT: Tuttle, 2018.

_____. *Kendo: Culture of the Sword.* Berkeley: University of California Press, 2016.

Cleary, Thomas. *Training the Samurai Mind: A Bushido Sourcebook.* Boston: Shambhala, 2009.

Conlan, Thomas. "Largesse and the Limits of Loyalty in the Fourteenth Century." *The Origins of Japan's Medieval World* (ed. Jeffrey P. Mass), pp. 39–64. Redwood City, CA: Stanford University Press, 1997.

Discover Japan (ed.). *Bujinesu ni Ikasu Bushido no Oshie.* Ei Shuppansha, 2015.

Friday, K. "Valorous Butchers: The Art of War during the Golden Age of the Samurai." *Japan Forum* 5 (1), 1993: pp. 1–19.

_____. "Bushido or Bull? A Medieval Historian's Perspective on the Imperial Army and the Japanese Warrior Tradition." *The History Teacher* 27, no. 3 (May 1994): pp. 339–349.

_____. *Legacies of the Sword.* Manoa: University of Hawai'i Press, 1997.

_____. *Samurai, Warfare and the State in Early Medieval Japan.* Abingdon, UK: Routledge, 2003.

Grafton, J. (Ed.), *101 Great Samurai Prints.* Mineola, NY: Dover, 2008.

Hayakawa Junzaburō (ed.), *Bujutsu Sosho.* Tokyo: Hachiman Shoten, 2003.

Ikegami, E. *The Taming of the Samurai: Honorific Individualism and the Making of Modern Japan.* Cambridge, MA: Harvard University Press, 1995.

Ikegami Ryota. *Zukai Sengoku Busho.* Tokyo: Shinkigensha, 2010.

Imamura Yoshio. *Nihon Budo Taikei.* Kyoto: Dohosha, 1982.

Inoue Tetsujiro (ed.). *Bushido Zensho,* Vols. 1-12. Tokyo: Kokusho Kankokai, 1998. (Reprint)

_____ and Sukemasa Arima (ed.). *Bushido Sosho,* Vols. 1-3. Tokyo: Hakubunkan, 1905.

Isogai Masayoshi and Hattori Harunori (ed.). *Koyo-gunkan,* 3 Vols. (*Sengoku Shiryo Sosho,* Vols. 3-5). Tokyo: Jinbutsu Oraisha, 1965, 1966.

Kaku Kōzo. *Miyamoto Musashi Jiten.* Tokyo: Tokyo-do, 2001.

Kishi Yuji. Kaku Kozo, *Zukai Zatsugaku Bushido.* Tokyo: Natsume-sha, 2006.

Maruyama Hiroyuki. *Zusetsu Muromachi Bakufu.* Tokyo: Ebisu Kosho Shuppan, 2018.

MdN Corporation. *Nihon no Rekishi: Sengoku Sozaishu,* 2010.

Mori Ryonosuke. *Zukai Bushido ga Yoku Wakaru.* Tokyo: Nihon Bungeisha, 2010.

_____. *Omoshiroi Hodo Yoku Wakaru Bushido.* Tokyo: Nihon Bungeisha, 2007.

Naramoto Tatsuya (et al). *Bijuaru-ban Taiyaku Bushido.* Tokyo: Mikasa Shobo, 2004.

Nitobe Inazo. *Bushido, the Soul of Japan: An Exposition of Japanese Thought.* Philadelphia: Leeds & Biddle, 1900.

Rogers John M. "Arts of War in Times of Peace, Swordsmanship" in *Honcho Bugei Shōden,* Chapter 6, in *Monumenta Nipponica,* Vol. 46-2, 1991, p. 173-202.

Sadler, A. L. *The Code of the Samurai.* North Clarendon, VT: Tuttle, 1988.

Sasama Yoshihiko. *Nihon Kassen Zuten.* Tokyo: Yuzankaku, 2017.

_____. *Nihon Budo Jiten.* Tokyo: Kashiwa Shobo, 1982.

_____. *Zusetsu Nihon Kassen Bugu Jiten.* Tokyo: Kashiwa Shobo, 2004.

_____. *Zusetsu Nihon Senjin Saho Jiten.* Tokyo: Kashiwa Shobo, 2000.

Takemitsu Makoto. *Nihonjin Nara Shitte Okitai Bushido.* Tokyo: Kawade Shobo, 2011.

_____. *Mikka de Wakaru Nihonshi.* Tokyo: Daiyamondo-sha, 2010.

Uozumi Takashi. *Miyamoto Musashi, "Heihō no Michi" wo Ikiru.* Tokyo: Iwanami Shoten, 2008.

_____. *Miyamoto Musashi, Nihonjin no michi.* Tokyo: Perikansha, 2002.

_____. *Teihon, Gorin-no-sho.* Tokyo: Shin Jinbutsu Ōraisha, 2005.

Van Straelen, H. *Yoshida Shoin: Forerunner of the Meiji Restoration.* Leiden, NLD: E.J. Brill, 1952.

Wilson William Scott. *The Book of Five Rings.* Tokyo: Kodansha International, 2001.

_____. *The Life-Giving Sword, Secret Teachings from the House of the Shogun, The Classic Text on Zen and the No-Sword by Musashi's Great Rival.* Tokyo: Kodansha International, 2003.

_____. *The Unfettered Mind, Writings of the Zen Master to the Sword Master.* Tokyo: Kodansha International, 1986.

_____. *Ideals of the Samurai: Writings of Japanese Warriors.* Santa Clarita, CA: Black Belt Communications, Inc., 1982.

Yamamoto Hirofumi. *Bushido no Meicho.* Tokyo: Chuokoron Shinsha, 2013

_____. *Bushido to Nihonjin no Kokoro.* Seishin Shuppansha, 2015.

_____. *Nihonjin no Kokoro Bushido Nyumon.* Tokyo: Kadokawa, 2014.

_____. *Zukai Bushido no koto ga Omoshiroi Hodo Wakaru Hon.* Tokyo: Chukei Shuppan, 2004.

Index

ABOUT TUTTLE
"Books to Span the East and West"

Our core mission at Tuttle Publishing is to create books which bring people together one page at a time. Tuttle was founded in 1832 in the small New England town of Rutland, Vermont (USA). Our fundamental values remain as strong today as they were then—to publish best-in-class books informing the English-speaking world about the countries and peoples of Asia. The world has become a smaller place today and Asia's economic, cultural and political influence has expanded, yet the need for meaningful dialogue and information about this diverse region has never been greater. Since 1948, Tuttle has been a leader in publishing books on the cultures, arts, cuisines, languages and literatures of Asia. Our authors and photographers have won numerous awards and Tuttle has published thousands of books on subjects ranging from martial arts to paper crafts. We welcome you to explore the wealth of information available on Asia at **www.tuttlepublishing.com**.

Published by Tuttle Publishing, an imprint of Periplus Editions (HK) Ltd.

www.tuttlepublishing.com

Text and diagrams Copyright © 2019
Alexander Bennett
Illustrations Copyright © 2019
Baptiste Tavernier except pages 4, 24, 29, 39, 41, 42, 53, 63, 92, 93, 94, 95, 112, 124, 137, 151 by the author, or otherwise noted.

Library of Congress Cataloging-in-Publication Data is in process.

ISBN: 978-4-8053-1507-1
First edition
22 21 20 19   6 5 4 3 2 1
Printed in Malaysia   1910VP

Distributed by

North America, Latin America & Europe
Tuttle Publishing
364 Innovation Drive, North Clarendon,
VT 05759-9436, USA
Tel: 1 (802) 773 8930
Fax: 1 (802) 773 6993
info@tuttlepublishing.com
www.tuttlepublishing.com

Japan
Tuttle Publishing
Yaekari Building, 3rd Floor
5-4-12 Osaki, Shinagawa-ku,
Tokyo 141-0032
Tel: (81) 3 5437 0171
Fax: (81) 3 5437 0755
sales@ tuttle.co.jp
www.tuttle.co.jp

Asia Pacific
Berkeley Books Pte Ltd
3 Kallang Sector #04-01
Singapore 349278
Tel: (65) 6741 2178
Fax: (65) 6741 2179
inquiries@periplus.com.sg
www.periplus.com